Science Activities A to Z

Join us on the web at

EarlyChildEd.delmar.com

Joanne Matricardi
Jeanne McLarty

THOMSON

DELMAR LEARNING

Australia Canada Mexico Singapore Spain United Kingdom United States

THOMSON

DELMAR LEARNING

Science Activities A to Z
Joanne Matricardi and Jeanne McLarty

Vice President, Career Education SBU:
Dawn Gerrain

Director of Editorial:
Sherry Gomoll

Acquisitions Editor:
Erin O'Connor

Editorial Assistant:
Stephanie Kelly

Director of Production:
Wendy A. Troeger

Production Editor:
Joy Kocsis

Production Assistant:
Angela Iula

Director of Marketing:
Wendy E. Mapstone

Cover Design:
Joseph Villanova

Composition:
Pre-Press Company, Inc.

Cover Image:
©Getty Images

Library of Congress Cataloging-in-Publication Data

Matricardi, Joanne.
  Science activities A to Z / Joanne Matricardi and Jeanne McLarty.
    p. cm. — (Activities A to Z series)
  Includes bibliographical references and index.
  ISBN-13 978-1-4018-7232-8
  ISBN-10 1-4018-7232-8
  (alk. paper)
  1. Science—Study and teaching (Early childhood) 2. Early childhood education—Activity programs. I. McLarty, Jeanne. II. Title.
  LB1139.5.S35M29 2005
  372.3'5—dc22

2004024064

NOTICE TO THE READER

Contents

Preface

This resource book is designed for preschool teachers, families of young children, and early childhood students. Science provides a wealth of developmental opportunities. Cognitive development is stimulated as children make predictions and investigate. Fine motor skills are enhanced when children participate in hands-on activities. Social development is encouraged as children work together sharing materials, and sensory exploration promotes emotional processing. *Science Activities A to Z* provides all these opportunities and more.

Science Activities A to Z is beneficial for families as they share in their children's process of discovery. The activities are fun and easy to do. Parents will find that most of the supplies and equipment needed are found in the kitchen or laundry room.

This book benefits early childhood students. Many student teachers are not enthusiastic about teaching science because they grew up without the benefit of hands-on experiences. *Science Activities A to Z* provides a plethora of activities that will bring joy to the science process. Activities are written in an easy-to-read, detailed, lesson plan format that will further aid those new to the teaching profession.

To enable children to practice predicting and to develop communication skills, you must ask open-ended questions. A closed-ended question leads to a one-word response. An open-ended question allows the child to think and answer creatively. An example of an open-ended question that encourages predicting is "What will happen when we mix red and blue together?" This type of question leaves a wondrous possibility of answers for the child. The closed-ended counterpart would ask, "Will we get purple when we mix red and blue together?" This question stifles the child's thinking and language, because the only responses possible are "Yes," "No," or the dreaded "I don't know."

The activities in this book yield three types of results. One is immediate: the children will witness changes in the process at one sitting. This is effective for children with very short attention spans. We must encourage children to have patience and to tolerate delayed gratification, however. The second type of activity yields short-term results; changes are not immediate but are seen over the course of one or several days. "Aromatherapy" takes two hours, and "Bouncing Egg" takes two or three days. Finally, long-term activities (such as "Evaporation") can take several weeks to yield results. You will want to alternate the type of activities you do. Children often need to see the immediate effects of what they're working on. Yet patience and perseverance must be encouraged. Using short-term and long-term activities will help meet this goal.

In each lesson plan, an "Ages" section suggests age appropriateness for that activity. When looking at the recommended age range, please consider the abilities of your children, their attention span, the adult-to-child ratio, and the materials to be used. Knowing your children, feel free to do experiments outside the suggested age ranges.

The "Group Size" section in each plan recommends the number of children to include in that activity. This, too, will depend on the materials, attention span, and knowledge of the children. Materials that are limited in number or those that present a safety consideration may require the activity to be limited to a single child or a very small group. Children must exhibit a longer attention span to work in a larger group. They need to be able to share materials and patiently wait their turns while observing others. If the activity can be done in a small group, use the children's age as a basis for the *maximum* number of children involved (e.g., two-year-olds, two in a group; three-year-olds, three in a group). As children begin to turn five-years-old the group size may be increased. Some teachers prefer to do specific experiments with the entire class, such as at group time, and then allow the children to engage in the same activity in smaller groups. Use knowledge of the children's abilities, interests, and attention span as a basis for determining the number of children involved at one time.

Other sections in the lesson plans include "Developmental Goals," "Learning Objective," "Materials," "Adult Preparation," and "Procedures." "Developmental Goals" are a description of the benefits the child derives from the science process. The "Learning Objective" is a behavioral statement of the child's use of certain materials to accomplish the immediate goal of the lesson. The "Materials" section aids the teacher or family in gathering all supplies needed for the activity. "Adult Preparation" details the work to be done before the child becomes involved in the process; older children are welcome to share this experience, however. "Procedures" are sequential steps for successfully engaging in the activity. Some activities also include "Notes," "Expansions," and "Activity Suggestions." These provide insights into the experience to ensure success or provide variances in techniques to produce different outcomes.

"Safety Precautions" are included with some of the activities, to alert the adult working with very young children that small items used may present a choking hazard, or that the adult should maintain close supervision due to other potential dangers. For instance, some activities involve the use of heat. Please supervise children closely when using these lesson plans.

This book contains two indexes. Teachers may refer to the "Science Concepts Index" when they want to focus on a specific science concept. The second (theme-specific) index is provided to assist adults in finding activities to complement traditional units used with young children. For example, "Bouncing Eggs" is listed under the "Farm" theme and is also included under "Nursery Rhymes" because it may be used when discussing Humpty Dumpty.

Science Activities A to Z sometimes includes food items in the materials needed for certain activities. Some of the products are edible and may be used as a snack. Others, such as the "Ultimate Egg Tester," explore the safety of using expired eggs. Some centers' policies may not permit the use of foods in classroom activities. Please check guidelines and follow your school's directives.

Science is a cognitive, creative process. It is important to use the activities you enjoy. Children can sense and mirror your enthusiasm. Have fun as you experiment together!

ANCILLARY MATERIAL

ONLINE COMPANION™

An Online Companion™ is an accompaniment to *Science Activities A to Z*. This site contains additional hands-on science activities for young children. The activites are also written in a lesson plan format. These detailed plans include developmental goals, a learning objective, a list of materials, adult preparation, a step-by-step procedure for the child, suggested group size, and age appropriateness. The activites are easy to understand and implement, either in the preschool classroom or at home.

The *Science Activities A to Z* Online Companion™ also provides links to related preschool sites. These links contain science ideas, supplies, and materials. Please visit www.earlychildhooded.delmar.com to gain access to this Online Companion™.

ACKNOWLEDGMENTS

This book is an accumulation of original and shared ideas developed over 40 years of teaching young children. Many thanks to our coworkers, students, and their parents for sharing and experimenting with us.

We would like to express our appreciation of Terry McLarty, our technical advisor. Thanks also go to Danielle Matricardi and Betty Somermeyer for their contributions.

We, and the editors at Thomson Delmar Learning, would also like to thank the following reviewers for their time, effort, and thoughtful contributions which helped to shape the final text:

Patricia Capistron
Rocking Unicorn Preschool
West Chatham, MA

Mary Hornbeck
Special Beginnings
Lenexa, KS

Jody Martin
Crème de la Crème
Golden, CO

Marilyn Rice, M.Ed.
Tuckaway Child Development
Richmond, VA

Brenda Schin
Child Care Consultant
Ballston Spa, NY

Joanne Matricardi
Jeanne McLarty

HELPFUL HINTS

Through years of experience, we've developed techniques that help our activities go more smoothly. Some are simple tricks to make cleanup easier. Others are strategies to ensure an activity's success. We routinely use the following procedures in our classrooms.

- ✄ Liquid watercolors may be used in place of food coloring. The colors are brilliant and eliminate the difficulty of mixing to achieve different hues. Liquid watercolors are also washable, whereas food coloring stains hands and clothing. Liquid watercolors may be ordered through a school supply catalog.

- ✄ Children should wear smocks when using food coloring or liquid watercolors.

- ✄ When using food coloring, you may first dilute it. Put 2 tablespoons water in a small bowl or cup. Add food coloring and stir.

- ✄ Recycle plastic snack-size applesauce and fruit cups. They are the perfect size for activities when full-size cups are not needed.

- ✄ If there is no sink in your classroom, have paper towels and a bucket of warm soapy water ready for easy cleanup.

- ✄ To label children's science experiments, write with a permanent marker directly on disposable products. If you are using kitchen cups or glasses, write the name on masking tape, then put the tape on the container. Make sure to remove the tape before washing the glasses. Failure to remove the tape may result in tape residue baking on glasses when they are washed and dried in a dishwasher.

✂ If possible, invest in a smooth-edge can opener to remove can lids without leaving sharp edges. If a smooth-edged can opener is not available, tape sharp edges of cans with masking tape before using them for experiments. Use the lids for magnetic projects only if the can has been cut with a smooth-edge can opener.

✂ Some preschools also serve one- and two-year-olds, and some activities can be adapted for use with younger children. Science with toddlers requires different management skills, however. The teacher of one-year-olds is often called away from the science table to attend to individual children. As a safety and cleanliness measure, we have found that putting all of a toddler's science supplies on a tray solves most problems. The tray is set on the table in front of the child, and when that child is finished and needs assistance washing hands, the teacher simply sets the tray up out of reach until ready for the next child.

SUPPLIES NEEDED

Most early childhood programs operate on a limited budget. Many of the materials we use in this book may be purchased at your local dollar store. The shopping list that follows is for use in buying supplies from dollar, grocery, hardware, office, school, and other discount stores. Also included is a family letter requesting recycled and household items.

SHOPPING LIST

Adult mittens or gloves
Aluminum cookie sheets
Aluminum foil
Animal cards
Animals (plastic)
Aquarium gravel
Assortment of small balls
Baking powder
Baking soda
Balancing scale
Bath towels
Balloons
Birdseed
Blank audiotapes
Blocks
Borax
Bottled water
Bowls
Brushes
Bubble wands
Bucket
Candy thermometer
Cellophane (blue, red, and yellow)
Child-size pitcher
Child-size watering can
Clear contact paper
Coffee cans (gallon)
Coffee filters (large)
Colander
Combs
Construction paper
Contact paper
Copy paper
Corn syrup
Cornstarch
Cotton balls
Cotton swabs
Craft sticks
Crayons (various brands)

Dawn®dish soap
Dinosaur pictures
Dried lima beans
Eyedroppers
Feathers
Flashlight (large)
Foam cups
Food coloring
Forks (metal)
Funnels
Glitter
Glass (clear, 12 oz.)
Glycerin
Goggles (child and adult sizes)
Hair picks
Hammer (child-size)
Heavy duty thread
Hook and loop tape
Hot Glue gun and glue sticks
Hot plate
Iron
Joy®dish soap
Kitchen strainers (small)
Knife
Large toothed combs
Liquid watercolors
Long wooden skewers
Magnetic marbles
Magnetic wand
Magnifying glasses (various styles)
Markers (permanent)
Markers (water-based)
Masking tape (regular and wide)
Measuring cup (glass with spout)
Measuring cups (small, plastic with spout)
Measuring spoons

Measuring tape (cloth)
Measuring tape (metal)
Metal muffin tin
Metal spatula
Ounce scale
Packaging tape
Paintbrushes
Pan (small)
Paper clips (metal)
Paper lunch bags
Paper towels
Paper umbrellas (from party store)
Paring knife
Pencils
Pennies
Pinecones
Plastic eggs
Plastic knives (sturdy)
Plastic spoons
Plastic straws
Plates (foam)
Plates (paper)
Plates (unbreakable)
Pom-poms
Popcorn
Poster board
Resealable plastic bags
Resealable plastic freezer bags
Rice
Roofing nails
Rubber bands
Rubbing alcohol
Ruler
Safety pins
Salt
Sand
Sandwich bags
Sanitary gloves
Saucepan

Scissors
Scoop
Screws
Sequins
Shaving cream
Slow cooker
Small containers (with secure lids)
Small fishnets (aquarium size)
Small spray bottles
Smocks
Smooth-edge can opener
Sponges
Spoons (long-handled)
Spoons (metal)
Squeeze containers
Stencils
Stethoscopes
Stickers
String
Tape recorder-player
Thermometer
Tin cans and lids
Tiny seashells
Tissue paper
Toothbrushes
Toothpaste
Toothpicks
Trays
Utility knife
Vegetable oil
Vinegar
Warming tray
Washer (large, flat, thin ring)
Wax paper
Whisk
White school glue
White vinegar
Wiggle eyes
Wooden blocks
Yarn

® The Procter & Gamble Company. Used by Permission.

FAMILY LETTER

Dear Families,

Many of the items we use in our science center may be found at home. Please save the following circled items and have your child bring them to school.

2-liter soda bottles	Fabric dye
20-ounce soda bottles	Flavored gelatin
35mm film canisters with lids	Flour
Aluminum cookie sheets	Foam cups
Aluminum foil	Fresh green leaves
Apples	Grass seeds
Assorted plastic lids	Ground cinnamon
Black tea	Hair dryer with cool-air setting
Blindfold (scarf)	Ice cream buckets
Box of tissues	Ice cube tray
Burlap	Insulated cooler
Cabbage (purple)	Jars (glass)
Can of food (unopened)	Jars (plastic)
Carbonated beverage	Jars (tall, narrow)
Celery	Jelly beans
Cleaned chicken or turkey bones	Large cotton or acrylic socks
Clear carbonated beverage	Leaves
Coffee	Lemons
Coffee cans	Lemon juice
Cork	Liquid flavoring
Corn syrup	Lollipop sticks
Cornmeal	Metal muffin tins
Cornstarch (16 oz. box)	Milk caps
Corrugated cardboard	Mirror
Cotton balls	Mismatched gloves
Crackers	Mismatched socks
Dried lima beans	Newspapers
Dry ice	Nylon umbrella (child-size)
Dry ice	Oil (vegetable)
Easter grass	Packing peanuts (biodegradable or
Eggs (fresh)	regular)
Eggs (past expiration date)	Pans (assorted sizes)
Egg cartons (foam)	Paint shirts/smocks
Electric skillet	Peanut butter
Emory board	Pennies
Empty tin cans	Pepper

Pie pans (aluminum)
Pie pans (glass)
Plastic eggs
Plastic gallon milk jug
Plastic grocery bags
Plastic jars with wide mouth lids
Potatoes
Potting soil
Powdered spice (cinnamon, garlic,
    pepper)
Pretzel sticks
Raisins
Rice (uncooked)
Rocks
Sandpaper
Seeds
Shoebox with lid
Silk
Small plants (roots intact)
Snack-size fruit cups
Soil

Squeeze bottles
Sugar
Syrup
Tea
Tennis balls
Toilet tissue tube
Toothpicks
Towels
Twigs
Vase (tall, narrow)
Warming tray
Whipping cream
White icing
White T-shirts (prewashed)
Whole milk
Wire hangers
Wooden cutting board
Wooden skewers
Yarn
Yeast

Thanks for your help!

Sincerely,

Absorption

DEVELOPMENTAL GOALS:

✄ To recognize colors

✄ To practice inferring

LEARNING OBJECTIVE:

Using cornstarch, a spray bottle, coloring, and a comb, the child will observe the absorption of color.

MATERIALS:

Cornstarch (1 box)
9" by 13" pan
Small spray bottle
Liquid watercolor or
   food coloring
Water
Large-toothed comb
   or hair pick
Smock

ADULT PREPARATION:

1. Fill a 9" by 13" pan with cornstarch and level it with the comb or hair pick.
2. Put liquid watercolor or food coloring in a small spray bottle and mix it with water. The amount of coloring depends on the hue desired.

PROCEDURES:

1. Wearing a smock, the child sprays color over cornstarch.
2. Ask the child what color is on the cornstarch.
3. Ask the child, "What will happen if we run a comb over the color?"
4. Child uses the comb or hair pick to brush through the design, watching the color disappear as the cornstarch absorbs the color.

continued

Absorption continued

EXPANSION:

Place stencils or cutouts on the cornstarch. Spray over the stencils or cutouts. When they are removed, their outline will still be visible.

GROUP SIZE:

2–3 children

Acid or Alkaline

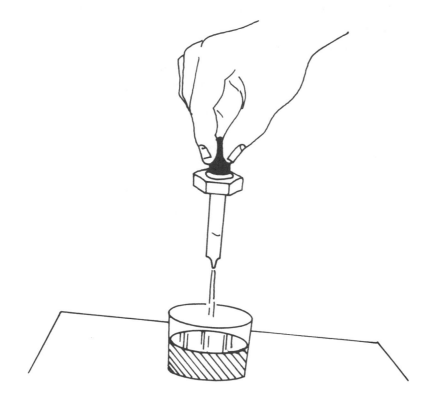

AGES: 3–5

DEVELOPMENTAL GOALS:

✂ To observe a chemical change

✂ To use small muscles

LEARNING OBJECTIVE:

Using purple cabbage juice, spoons, eyedroppers, vinegar, and baking soda, the child will observe solutions changing colors.

MATERIALS:

Purple cabbage
Knife to cut cabbage
Water
Pan
Stove or hot plate
Container
3 small clear cups
3 small bowls
2 small pieces of paper
Marker or pen
White vinegar
Baking soda
Bottled water
Measuring cup
Spoons
Eyedroppers
Paper towels

ADULT PREPARATION:

1. Cut purple cabbage into chunks.
2. Boil cabbage in 2 quarts of water. (Water will turn purple.)
3. Pour purple liquid into a container and let it cool.
4. When cool, cover with a lid.
5. Put vinegar, bottled water, and baking soda in separate bowls.
6. Write *vinegar* on one small piece of paper and *water* on another. Put each paper with the correct solution.
7. Fill three cups half full of the cooled purple solution.

PROCEDURES:

The child will complete the following steps, using spoons or eyedroppers:

1. Add white vinegar to the first cup.
2. Add bottled water to the second cup.
3. Add baking soda to the third cup.

continued

Acid or Alkaline continued

Notes: Vinegar (an acid) will turn the solution red. Plain bottled water will cause no change in the solution's color. Baking soda (an alkaline substance) will turn the solution blue or green. A less alkaline substance will turn the solution blue, and one that is more alkaline (i.e., that contains more baking soda) will turn it green. Mixing vinegar and baking soda solutions will cause a fizzing reaction, so be prepared with paper towels for cleanup.

EXPANSION:

Add baking soda to the vinegar-and-cabbage solution, which neutralize the vinegar, returning the solution to its original purple color. The reverse also works: add vinegar to the baking-soda-and-cabbage solution, and it will return to the original purple color.

GROUP SIZE:

3–4 children

4

Air

AGES: 3–5

DEVELOPMENTAL GOALS:

✄ To understand that air can move objects

✄ To make predictions

LEARNING OBJECTIVE:

Using a straw, cotton balls, milk caps, pennies, pencils, and a hair dryer, the child will move objects with air.

MATERIALS:

Plastic straws
Hair dryer
Cotton balls
Milk caps
Pennies
Pencils

ADULT PREPARATION:

1. Place the cotton balls on the table.

PROCEDURES:

1. The adult will hand the child an individual straw.
2. Using the straw, the child will blow the cotton balls across the table.
3. The adult will place heavier objects on the table, such as milk caps, pennies, pencils, etc.
4. Ask the child, "What will you be able to move by blowing air through the straw?"
5. The child will attempt to move the objects by blowing at them through the straw.
6. The child will use the hair dryer (with close supervision) to blow objects that would not move with the use of the straw.

Note: Empty squirt bottles may be used in place of the straws.

GROUP SIZE:

2–3 children

A

DEVELOPMENTAL GOALS:

✂ To observe insects

✂ To use a magnifying glass

LEARNING OBJECTIVE:

Using an ant farm and magnifying glass, the child will observe the movement of ants.

MATERIALS:

Ant farm kit
Ants
Magnifying glasses

Ants

ADULT PREPARATION:

1. Following directions provided, put ant farm together. (The directions will include care of the ants.)

PROCEDURES:

1. The child will observe ants with a magnifying glass.

ACTIVITY SUGGESTION:

Ant farms may be purchased from school supply stores, school supply catalog, or on-line.

GROUP SIZE:

2–3 children (each needs a magnifying glass)

Apples Turn Brown

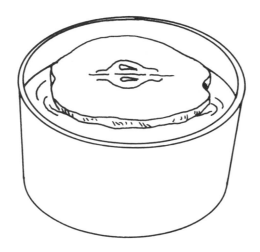

DEVELOPMENTAL GOALS:

✂ To observe objects using the senses

✂ To stimulate eye-hand coordination

LEARNING OBJECTIVE:

Use apples, plates, bowls of water, and lemon juice, the child will observe change.

MATERIALS:

Apple
Paring knife
Small bowl
Plates
Two mid-sized bowls
Water
Lemon juice
Measuring cup and spoon

ADULT PREPARATION:

1. Measure approximately 1 cup of water into each bowl.

2. Pour lemon juice into a small bowl.

3. Cut apple in half. Do not peel or core the apple. The cored area may create an air pocket when placed in the solutions, which will alter the results.

PROCEDURES:

The child will complete the following steps:

1. Measure 1 tablespoon of lemon juice and place it in one of the bowls with water. Do not add anything to the second bowl.

2. Place an apple half in each bowl so that the skinless part of the apple is covered with either the water or water-and-lemon-juice solution, and leave the apple halves in the solutions for several minutes.

continued

7

Apples Turn Brown continued

3. Remove apple halves from the bowls and set them on plates.

4. Watch as adult marks the apple half that came from the lemon-water solution.

5. Observe apple halves throughout the day, noting that the apple half soaked in plain water turns brown and the apple half soaked in lemon-water solution remains fresh looking.

Notes: The acid in lemon juice prevents the apple pieces from browning. Soaking in undiluted orange or pineapple juice will also prevent fruit from browning.

GROUP SIZE:

2–4 children

Aromatherapy

ADULT PREPARATION:

1. Pour 1 cup hot water into slow cooker. (Beginning with hot water hastens the cooking process.)
2. Plug the slow cooker in and turn it on high.
3. Wash the apples.
4. Peel and core the apples and cut them in half.
5. Put cinnamon in a small bowl.

PROCEDURES:

1. Using a plastic knife, the child will cut apples into small pieces.
2. The adult will add the pieces of fruit to the slow cooker.
3. The child will measure 1 teaspoon cinnamon.
4. The child will add cinnamon to the cooker and stir with the long-handled spoon.

Notes: Leave the lid off the cooker to maximize the scent; the aroma of cooked apples promotes a feeling of well-being. This process takes approximately two hours.

GROUP SIZE:

3–6 children

AGES: 3–5

DEVELOPMENTAL GOALS:

- ✂ To promote fine motor control
- ✂ To stimulate the sense of smell

LEARNING OBJECTIVE:

Use apples, cinnamon, a knife, and a slow cooker, the child will create a scent.

MATERIALS:

Slow cooker
Apples (one half for each child)
Ground cinnamon
Small bowl
Water
Measuring cup
Measuring spoon (teaspoon)
Sturdy plastic knives
Long-handled spoon

Auditory Discrimination

DEVELOPMENTAL GOALS:

- ✄ To improve auditory discrimination
- ✄ To recognize sounds made by certain animals or common objects

LEARNING OBJECTIVE:

Using a tape player, pictures, and a tape, the child will identify the sounds made by animals or objects seen in photographs.

MATERIALS:

Tape recorder-player
Blank audiotape
Pictures of animals or
   common objects

ADULT PREPARATION:

1. Using the tape recorder and a blank tape, record sounds of animals or common objects such as the phone ringing, a hairdryer, water running, etc. (This may be done in the classroom with the children present.)
2. Take pictures of the items you recorded or, using patterns, create silhouettes of the objects.
3. Set out pictures of the items you recorded.

PROCEDURES:

1. Show the children the pictures of animals or common objects.
2. Ask children to identify the pictures.
3. Play the sound tape for the class and ask children to identify the picture associated with each sound.

GROUP SIZE:

1–5 children

Bird Feeder

AGES: 2–5

DEVELOPMENTAL GOALS:

- ✂ To care for birds
- ✂ To develop small motor skills

LEARNING OBJECTIVE:

Using a pine cone, peanut butter, plastic knife, and birdseed, the child will create a bird feeder.

MATERIALS:

Pine cone
Peanut butter (use corn syrup if the child has peanut allergies)
Plate
Plastic knife or craft stick
Bowl
Birdseed
Spoon
Yarn or string
Scissors

ADULT PREPARATION:

1. Put birdseed in bowl.
2. Put pine cone on plate.
3. Put a spoonful of peanut butter on the plate.
4. Cut a 12" length of yarn or string.

PROCEDURES:

The child will complete the following steps:

1. Spread peanut butter on the pinecone with plastic knife or craft stick.
2. Using a spoon, pour birdseed on the pine cone (birdseed will stick to it).
3. With adult help, tie the yarn or string to the pine cone and hang the bird feeder outside.

GROUP SIZE:

1–3 children

Bouncing Egg

DEVELOPMENTAL GOALS:

✄ To observe a transformation

✄ To interact with an adult

LEARNING OBJECTIVE:

Using an egg, cup, and vinegar, the child will observe a transformation of an egg shell.

MATERIALS:

Raw eggs
Clear plastic cups
White vinegar
Child-size pitcher
Tray
Permanent marker
Masking tape
Paper towels for cleanup
Bucket of soapy water if
    sink is not available

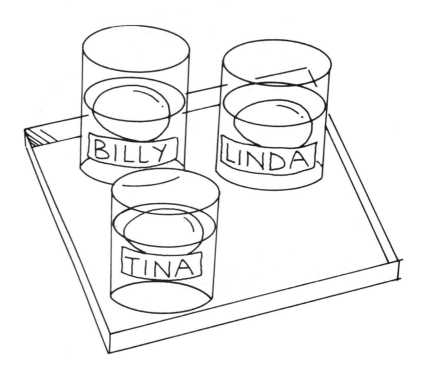

ADULT PREPARATION:

1. Pour vinegar into a child-size pitcher.
2. Write each child's name on masking tape and place the tape on individual cups.

PROCEDURES:

1. The child will carefully put a raw egg into a clear plastic cup.
2. The child will pour vinegar over the egg, totally submerging it. (While the egg sits in its cup in a safe place for 48–72 hours, the shell of the egg will dissolve, leaving a rubbery egg.)
3. The adult will pour the vinegar off the egg.
4. The adult will demonstrate how to drop the egg onto a tray, holding the egg only two inches above the tray.

continued

Bouncing Egg continued

5. The child will carefully drop the egg onto the tray from a height of two inches and will watch the egg bounce.

6. The child will drop the egg from successively greater heights until the egg breaks.

Note: Be sure to wash hands in soapy water after this activity.

GROUP SIZE:

1–3 children

Bubbles

AGES: 2¹/₂–5

DEVELOPMENTAL GOALS:

- ✂ To coordinate large and small muscles
- ✂ To enhance social development

LEARNING OBJECTIVE:

Using dish soap, glycerin, and a large bubble wand, the child will take turns creating bubbles.

MATERIALS:

Glycerin (purchased in pharmaceutical departments)
Joy® or Dawn® dish soap (experiment will not work with other detergents)
Water
Measuring cup
Measuring spoon (tablespoon)
Large container
Bubble wands
Wire coat hangers

® The Procter & Gamble Company. Used by Permission.

ADULT PREPARATION:

1. Fill a large container with 10 cups of water.
2. Bend wire coat hangers into various shapes to use as large bubble wands.

PROCEDURES:

1. Children will squirt 1 cup of Joy® or Dawn® detergent into a measuring cup.
2. Adult will add the dish soap to the container of water.
3. Adult will measure 3–4 tablespoons of glycerin and put it in the container of water.
4. Children will take turns stirring the mixture gently with a large spoon.
5. Children will take turns dipping coat hanger wands into the bubble solution.
6. Children will wave wands to create large bubbles.

continued

Bubbles continued

Notes: Traditional bubble wands may also be used in the bubble solution. To avoid evaporation on very dry days, add a little more water to offset evaporation. If you try this with other detergents the results may vary.

⚠ SAFETY PRECAUTION:

Store glycerin out of the reach of children. When ingested in large amounts, it can cause gastrointestinal problems.

GROUP SIZE:

If done outside, this may be used with the entire class. All may squirt some dish soap in the measuring cup, all may stir the bubble mixture and take turns dipping bubble wands into it. If done inside, the group may include as many children as can fit comfortably around a table.

Butter

AGES: 3–5 (This activity may be used with younger children. Their attention span may not last long enough to shake the cream into butter without adult assistance, however.)

DEVELOPMENTAL GOALS:

- ✂ To observe transformations
- ✂ To increase self-help skills

LEARNING OBJECTIVE:

Using whipping cream, a small container with a lid, and salt, the child will make butter.

MATERIALS:

Whipping cream
Small plastic containers with secure lids
Child-size pitcher
Small bowl
Salt
Crackers
Knife (plastic knife for younger children)
Plates

ADULT PREPARATION:

1. Put whipping cream into a small pitcher that child can successful pour with.
2. Put salt in a small bowl.
3. Place crackers on plate.

PROCEDURES:

The child will complete the following steps:

1. Wash hands.
2. Pour whipping cream into the small container until it is approximately half full.
3. Add a pinch of salt.
4. Watch as adult fastens lid on tightly.
5. Shake container until the cream thickens into butter.
6. Spread the butter on crackers with knife.

continued

Butter continued

Notes: Butter is created because the cream has fat and protein. When you shake the jar, the fat and protein stick together.

If the container is round and unbreakable with a secure lid, this activity may be done at circle time, where the children roll the container on the floor from child to child.

GROUP SIZE:

1–5 children

Butterfly

AGES: 3–5

DEVELOPMENTAL GOALS:

- ✂ To increase creativity
- ✂ To gain fine motor control

LEARNING OBJECTIVE:

Using butterfly pattern, paper bags, crayons, markers, stickers, craft sticks, pom-poms, google eyes, and glue, the child will create a caterpillar and enact its transformation into a butterfly.

MATERIALS:

Brown paper bags— lunch size (one for each child)
Butterfly patterns (one for each child)
Crayons
Markers
Stickers
Craft sticks (one for each child)
Pom-poms
Wiggle eyes
White school glue

ADULT PREPARATION:

1. Make cutouts of butterflies that will fit into paper lunch bags.

PROCEDURES:

1. Child decorates butterfly with stickers, markers, and crayons.
2. Child glues pom-poms and google eyes on a craft stick, creating a caterpillar.
3. After allowing the caterpillar to dry, the child hides butterfly in the paper bag.
4. Adult explains that the paper bag is like the cocoon that the caterpillar spins.
5. Child places caterpillar in paper bag.
6. Adult explains that the caterpillar will turn into a beautiful butterfly while in the cocoon.

continued

Butterfly continued

7. Child pulls butterfly out of the paper bag.

8. Child retells the story on his or her own while reenacting the transformation.

GROUP SIZE:

3–4 children

Carbonated Raisins

AGES: 2–5

DEVELOPMENTAL GOALS:

- ✂ To improve observation skills
- ✂ To enlarge vocabulary

LEARNING OBJECTIVE:

Using raisins, clear carbonated beverages, a teaspoon, and a clear glass the child will observe raisins moving up and down.

MATERIALS:

Clear carbonated beverage
Clear glass
Raisins
Small bowl
Measuring spoon (teaspoon)

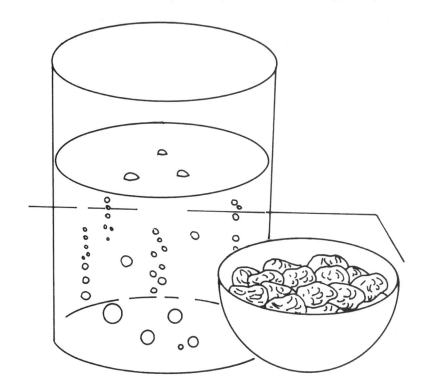

ADULT PREPARATION:

1. Put raisins in a small bowl.
2. Wait for children to sit down before opening the carbonated beverage. (Activity will not work if the beverage is flat.)

PROCEDURES:

The child will complete the following steps:

1. Measure a teaspoon of raisins and put the raisins into a glass.
2. Pour in clear carbonated beverage to a level 4"–6" high.
3. Observe the raisins moving up and down and describe what they are doing.

Notes: Bubbles of carbon dioxide form around each raisin, lifting them to the surface where the bubbles break, releasing carbon dioxide into the air. Gravity then pulls the raisins to the bottom where bubbles form again, lifting them back to the top.

GROUP SIZE:

2–5 children

20

Celery

ADULT PREPARATION:

1. Cut the base off a stalk of celery. Leave the leaves attached.
2. Put water in a child-size pitcher.

PROCEDURES:

1. Wearing a smock, child pours water into a cup, filling it two-thirds full.
2. Child adds food coloring and stirs with a spoon.
3. Adult asks, "What will happen to the celery when we add it to the tinted water?"
4. Child puts celery in the water, placing the bottom of the celery all the way in the water and leaving the top half above the water line, with leaves rising above the cup.
5. Adult or child writes the child's name with permanent marker on a piece of masking tape and places it on the cup.

continued

AGES: 2–5

DEVELOPMENTAL GOALS:

✂ To make predictions
✂ To compare objects

LEARNING OBJECTIVE:

Using celery, water, food coloring, a cup, and spoon, the child will observe how the veins in the celery absorb water.

MATERIALS:

Stalk of celery
Water
Food coloring (dark colors work best)
Tray
Cup (one for each child)
Child-size pitcher
Spoon
Knife
Permanent marker
Masking tape
Smock

Celery continued

6. Child puts the cup on a tray.

7. Adult places the tray safely out of reach.

8. Adult shows celery to the children each day and asks, "How is the celery different than it was yesterday?"

Notes: It will take two or three days for the leaves to become tinted with color. The trail of color shows how the plant absorbs the water through its "veins."

GROUP SIZE:

1–2 children

Chlorophyll

ADULT PREPARATION:

1. Pick fresh green leaves.
2. Place a sheet of paper on the cutting board or piece of wood and another sheet of paper nearby.

PROCEDURES:

The child will complete the following steps:

1. Place a fresh green leaf on the paper.
2. Put a sheet of paper on top of the leaf.
3. Pound the top sheet of paper with the hammer, on the spot that covers the leaf.
4. Lift the paper to see the green color on both sheets of paper, which resulted when chlorophyll was pounded out of the leaf.

SAFETY PRECAUTION:

When using a hammer, limit the activity to one child at a time to prevent injuries.

GROUP SIZE:

1 child

AGES: 2–5

DEVELOPMENTAL GOALS:

- ✄ To increase large-muscle development
- ✄ To delight in movement and rhythm

LEARNING OBJECTIVE:

Using a fresh green leaf, white paper, wooden cutting board, and hammer, the child will transfer chlorophyll from the leaf to the paper.

MATERIALS:

Fresh green leaves
White paper
Wooden cutting board or a piece of wood
Child-size hammer
Paper

C

Color Mix

DEVELOPMENTAL GOALS:

- ✄ To understand color mixing
- ✄ To improve fine muscle skills

LEARNING OBJECTIVE:

Using food coloring, icing, pretzel sticks, and a plate, the child will use primary colors to mix secondary colors.

MATERIALS:

Red, yellow, and blue food coloring
Can of white icing (One can is enough for 12 children.)
Paper plates (one for each child)
Pretzel sticks (three for each child)
Spoon
Smock

ADULT PREPARATION:

1. Put a spoonful of icing in three separate piles on each plate.

PROCEDURES:

The child will complete the following steps:

1. Wearing a smock, place a drop of food coloring in each pile of icing, making one pile red, one yellow, and one blue.
2. Mix the icing with pretzel sticks, using one pretzel stick for each color.
3. Mix the different colors of icing together to make new colors.

GROUP SIZE:

1–5 children

24

Color Windows

ADULT PREPARATION:

1. Cut the centers out of six paper plates.
2. Cut a cellophane circle that will fit inside the paper plate—one from each color.
3. Cover the hole of the first plate with the blue cellophane circle. Tape it to the plate.
4. Glue the second plate over the first so that the two plates fit flat together, with the cellophane visible between the holes.
5. Repeat steps 3–4 with yellow and red cellophane.
6. Allow glue to dry.

PROCEDURES:

1. Child views classroom through the colored cellophane plate.
2. Ask the child, "What will happen if we put two different plates together?"
3. Child puts two different plates together and notices the color change.

GROUP SIZE:

1–5 children

AGES: 1–5

DEVELOPMENTAL GOALS:

- To mix colors to create new colors
- To practice inferring

LEARNING OBJECTIVE:

Using cellophane and paper plates, the child will view his or her surroundings through different colors.

MATERIALS:

Red, blue, and yellow cellophane
Six paper plates
Scissors
Tape
Glue

Crystals

AGES: 3–5

DEVELOPMENTAL GOALS:

✄ To observe a transformation

✄ To interact with an adult

LEARNING OBJECTIVE:

Using borax, water, string, a paper clip, a craft stick, a jar, spoon, and measuring cup, the child will make crystals.

MATERIALS:

Hot plate
Small pan
Bath towels
Spoon
Borax (purchased in the laundry aisle)
Water
Large bowl for water
Medium bowl for borax
String
Paper clip or safety pin
Craft stick
Glass jar (pint size)
Measuring cup
Permanent marker
Masking tape

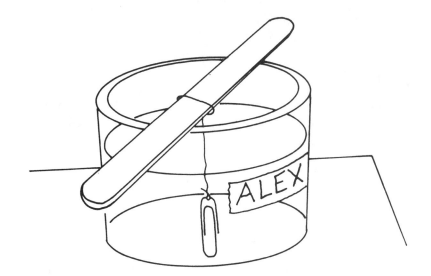

ADULT PREPARATION:

1. Put water in a large bowl.
2. Put borax in bowl.
3. Set pan on the hot plate.

PROCEDURES:

1. Child dips measuring cup into large bowl of water and measures 1 cup water, then pours the water into the pan.
2. Adult measures ¼ cup borax and places it in pint-size jar.
3. When water comes to a boil, adult pours it into the jar.
4. Adult carefully stirs the mixture with a spoon until the borax is dissolved.
5. With adult help, child ties one end of string to the middle of a craft stick and other end of string to paper clip or safety pin (to weight the string so it will hang straight).

continued

Crystals continued

6. Child lowers the paper clip end of the string into the jar so that the string reaches toward the bottom of the jar but does not touch the bottom.

7. Child lays craft stick across top of jar.

Notes: As the mixture cools, crystals will form and attach themselves to the string. Crystals will be fully formed by the next day.

ACTIVITY SUGGESTION:

A colored pipe cleaner may be used in place of the string. The color will show through the crystals, making them appear to be the color of the pipe cleaner.

SAFETY PRECAUTIONS:

Close supervision is required when working with a hot plate and boiling water. Store borax and other detergents out of the reach of children.

GROUP SIZE:

1 child

Curds and Whey

AGES: 3–5

DEVELOPMENTAL GOALS:

✂ To practice cooking procedures

✂ To improve use of language

LEARNING OBJECTIVE:

Using whole milk, lemon juice, spoon, salt, measuring cup, tablespoon, sauce pan, hot plate, and colander, the child will make curds and whey.

MATERIALS:

Sauce pan
Hot plate
Bath towels
Whole milk
Lemon juice
Stirring spoon
Salt
Measuring cup
Measuring spoon
  (tablespoon)
Child-size pitcher
Bowl for lemon juice
Small bowl for salt
Individual spoons
Colander with fine
  mesh or very tiny
  holes

ADULT PREPARATION:

1. Wrap towels around hot plate for safety purposes. The towels are on the outside of the appliance.
2. Put milk in a small pitcher to enable the child to pour it.
3. Put lemon juice in bowl.
4. Put salt in a small bowl.

PROCEDURES:

The child will complete the following steps:

1. Wash hands.
2. Recite the nursery rhyme "Little Miss Muffet": "Little Miss Muffet sat on a tuffet, eating her curds and whey. Along came a spider who sat down beside her and frightened Miss Muffet away."
3. Pour milk into measuring cup, measuring 1 full cup.
4. Pour milk into saucepan.

continued

Curds and Whey continued

5. Measure 1 tablespoon of lemon juice and add it to pan.

6. Watch as adult places pan on hot plate over medium heat.

7. With adult assistance, stir the mixture occasionally. (As it heats, the lemon juice will curdle the milk, resulting in curds. The liquid that remains is whey.)

8. Add a pinch of salt and stir.

9. Watch as adult drains the whey from the curds, using a fine mesh colander, and reserves some whey for tasting.

10. Place spoonfuls of curds on a plate, with adult assistance, and place in the refrigerator to cool.

11. Taste the curds and whey, using a spoon.

Notes: Children who taste this mixture give it mixed reviews. Some do not like it, but others ask for more. Discuss with children the taste of the curds and whey. Lead the discussion by asking if it is sweet, sour, or salty.

Skim milk may be substituted for whole milk. Children prefer the taste of whole milk, yet it produces curds of very fine texture. Using skim milk results in coarser curds.

 SAFETY PRECAUTION:
Supervise children closely when using heating elements.

GROUP SIZE:

1–2 children

DEVELOPMENTAL GOALS:

- ✂ To make comparisons
- ✂ To participate in a group project

LEARNING OBJECTIVE:

Using string, tape, craft sticks, and pictures of dinosaurs, the child will comprehend the size of dinosaurs.

MATERIALS:

String
Measuring tape
Rulers
Masking tape
Permanent marker
Craft sticks
Pictures of a triceratops, a tyrannosaurus, and a brachiosaur

Dinosaur Measurement

TRICERATOPS 30 FT. LONG

ADULT PREPARATION:

1. Measure and cut strings the height and length of three dinosaurs: (a) For a triceratops, cut a string 30' long for its length and one 7' long for its height. (b) For a tyrannosaur, cut strings 40' long (length) and 15–20' long (height). (c) For a brachiosaur, cut strings 85' long (length) and 50' long (height).

2. Write the dinosaur's name and length or height on a piece of masking tape with a permanent marker. Place the tape on a ruler.

3. Wrap the string around the rulers.

continued

Dinosaur Measurement continued

PROCEDURES:

1. Outside or in a gym, the child holds one end of the string in place as the adult walks out the measurement of the dinosaur.

2. After adult walks as far as the string will reach, adult tapes each end of the string to the gym floor or parking lot. (If a grassy area is used, push craft sticks into the ground and tape the string to the craft sticks.)

3. Child or adult places the picture of the relevant dinosaur near the string designating its length.

4. The string length allows the child to observe what the size of the dinosaur would have been.

5. Steps 1–3 are repeated for other dinosaurs.

EXPANSION:

Compare the dinosaurs' sizes with those of people and other animals to give the children a realistic view of them. (A giraffe is 15–17' tall. The average person is 5–6' tall.)

GROUP SIZE:

10–15 children

D

AGES: 2–5

DEVELOPMENTAL GOALS:

✂ To discuss environmental practices

✂ To participate in a small group activity

LEARNING OBJECTIVE:

Using leaves, twigs, newspaper, coffee, detergent, toilet paper, kitchen strainers, coffee filters, small fishnets, and a large container of water, the child will pollute water and then attempt to clean it.

MATERIALS:

Large container
Water
Small fishnets
(aquarium-size)
Small kitchen strainers
Coffee filters
Twigs
Leaves
Newspaper
Coffee
Toilet paper
Oil (vegetable)
Detergent
Trashcan

Dirty Water

ADULT PREPARATION:

1. Put water in large container.
2. Gather leaves and twigs.

PROCEDURES:

The child will complete the following steps:

1. Help adult add leaves and twigs to the large container of water while adult explains that objects from nature fall into lakes and rivers.
2. Add pieces of newspaper to the water while adult explains that some people are careless and let their trash fall in the water.
3. Add coffee to the water while adult explains how spills run into lakes and rivers.
4. Add detergent and pieces of toilet paper to the water while learning that products from our homes end up in the water.
5. Use small kitchen strainer, fishnets, and coffee filters to clean the water, putting the items pulled out of the water into trashcan.

Notes: Ask the children what else they could do to totally clean the water. Discuss with the children the importance of keeping our lakes and rivers clean.

GROUP SIZE:

2–4 children

Dissolving Particles

AGES: 3–5

DEVELOPMENTAL GOALS:

- ✂ To increase self-help skills
- ✂ To improve observation skills

LEARNING OBJECTIVE:

Using cups, spoons, water, measuring cup, measuring spoon, salt, and sugar, the child will observe particles dissolving.

MATERIALS:

Four clear cups
Spoons for stirring
Water
Child-size pitcher
Small bowls
Glass measuring cup with pour spout
Measuring spoon (teaspoon)
Salt
Sugar

ADULT PREPARATION:

1. Put water in a child-size pitcher.
2. Put salt and sugar in separate small bowls.

PROCEDURES:

1. Child pours 1 cup of water into a measuring cup.
2. Adult heats the water in a microwave for 30 seconds, or until warm.
3. Child pours ½ cup of warm water into each of two cups.
4. Child pours ½ cup of cold tap water into each of two cups.
5. Child adds a teaspoon of salt to one of the cups containing cold water, and a teaspoon of salt to one cup containing warm water.
6. Child adds a teaspoon of sugar to one cup with cold water and a teaspoon of sugar to a cup with warm water.
7. Using separate spoons for salt and sugar mixtures, child stirs all cups, observing that the sugar dissolves faster than the salt and that both sugar and salt dissolve in cold and warm water.

GROUP SIZE:

3–4 children

D

DEVELOPMENTAL GOALS:

- ✂ To observe objects using the senses
- ✂ To improve fine muscle control

LEARNING OBJECTIVE:

Using measuring cups and spoons, water, salt, oil, flour, cornstarch, bowls, and spoons, the child will make dough.

MATERIALS:

Measuring cup
Measuring spoons
Water
Box of salt
Oil (vegetable)
Flour
Cornstarch
Food coloring or liquid
   watercolor (optional)
Smocks (if using food
   coloring)
Large bowl for mixing
Bowl for cornstarch
Large bowl for flour
Small bowl for oil
Spoon for stirring

Dough

ADULT PREPARATION:

1. Put water in a child-size pitcher.
2. Set salt box on table.
3. Pour oil into a bowl.
4. Put cornstarch in a bowl.
5. Put flour in a large bowl.

PROCEDURES:

1. Children wash hands before beginning the activity.
2. Children take turns measuring.
3. One child pours water into a measuring cup, measuring 1 full cup.
4. One child pours salt into a second measuring cup, measuring 1 full cup.
5. One child measures 2 teaspoons of oil.
6. Children take turns mixing all ingredients together in a bowl, with adult help if needed.
7. If colored dough is desired, a child wearing a smock adds food coloring or liquid watercolor before mixing.
8. Children measure 2½–3 cups of flour and 2 tablespoons of cornstarch and add the flour and cornstarch to the liquid and salt mixture.
9. Children take turns mixing the ingredients, with adult help.
10. When the mixture reaches a dough consistency, children pour it onto the table.
11. Adult divides the dough between the children.
12. Children knead dough and form it into desired shapes.

Notes: The recipe used in the procedures makes enough dough for four children to knead. Start with 2½ cups of flour. If the mixture is still sticky, add another ½ cup of flour. The recipe can be halved or doubled, tripled, and so on, depending on the size of the group.
The dough may be stored in resealable plastic bags.

GROUP SIZE:

2–4 children

34

Dry Ice

ADULT PREPARATION:

1. Wearing goggles and gloves, place the dry ice on a towel.
2. Fold the towel over the dry ice so the towel covers the ice.
3. Using a hammer, break the dry ice into smaller pieces.

PROCEDURES:

1. Ask the children, "What will happen if we put dry ice in a closed container?"
2. Wearing gloves, put a chip of dry ice into a film canister.
3. Put the lid on the canister and stand back. The lid will pop off the film canister.
4. Ask the children, "Why did the lid pop off the film canister?"
5. Explain that the evaporating carbon dioxide is a gas that expanded and forced the lid off the container.

continued

D

AGES: 3–5

DEVELOPMENTAL GOALS:

✂ To improve observation skills

✂ To make predictions

LEARNING OBJECTIVE:

Using dry ice and film canisters, the children will observe the dry ice popping the lid off the canister.

MATERIALS:

5 pounds dry ice
Insulated ice chest
Gloves or mittens
35 mm film canisters
Hammer
Goggles—adult size
Towels

35

Dry Ice continued

SAFETY PRECAUTIONS:

Dry ice is frozen carbon dioxide (−109 degrees F, −78.5 degrees C), and it can be dangerous. The following safety precautions are mandatory for working with dry ice:

1. Avoid contact with the skin.
2. Always use gloves when handling dry ice, because it can cause instant frostbite.
3. Do not use gloves if they become wet; the cold will go through the wet gloves.
4. Use in a well-ventilated area.

GROUP SIZE:

3–4 children

Dry Ice and Dish Soap

AGES: 3–5

DEVELOPMENTAL GOALS:

✂ To observe objects using the senses

✂ To improve social skills

LEARNING OBJECTIVE:

Using dry ice, water, and dish soap, the children will observe bubbles being created.

MATERIALS:

5 pounds dry ice
Insulated cooler
Gloves or mittens—adult size
Hammer
Goggles—adult size
Towels
Water
Clear plastic container
Dish soap

ADULT PREPARATION:

1. Wearing goggles and gloves, place the dry ice on a towel.
2. Fold the towel over the dry ice so the towel covers the ice.
3. Using a hammer, break the dry ice into smaller pieces.

PROCEDURES:

1. Ask the children, "What will happen if we put dish soap in with the dry ice and water?"
2. With the children's help, put water into a plastic container.
3. Wearing gloves, add a chunk of dry ice to the water.
4. Children may add dish soap to the water. The soap mixes with the evaporating carbon dioxide, causing bubbles to continually form and spill out of the container.
5. Under close supervision, the children may take turns popping the bubbles above the surface of the water.
6. Ask children to observe that, when the bubbles are popped, carbon dioxide escapes as steam.

continued

Dry Ice and Dish Soap continued

SAFETY PRECAUTIONS:

Dry ice is frozen carbon dioxide (–109 degrees F, –78.5 degrees C), and it can be dangerous. The following safety precautions are mandatory for working with dry ice:

1. Avoid contact with the skin.
2. Always use gloves when handling dry ice, because it can cause instant frostbite.
3. Do not use gloves if they become wet; the cold will go through the wet gloves.
4. Use in a well-ventilated area.

GROUP SIZE:

3–4 children

Erosion

AGES: 2–5

DEVELOPMENTAL GOALS:

✂ To introduce the word *erosion*

✂ To promote sharing by taking turns

LEARNING OBJECTIVE:

Using sand, a watering can, and water, the child will observe erosion.

MATERIALS:

Sensory table or large container
Sand
Water
Child-size watering can

ADULT PREPARATION:

1. Put sand in sensory table or a large container.
2. Moisten sand with water for easy molding.
3. Put water in a child-size watering can.

PROCEDURES:

1. Children help adult mold the sand into a hill.
2. Ask the children, "What will happen to the hill if we pour water on it?"
3. Children take turns pouring water on the hill.

Notes: The hill will erode or wash away. Discuss how rain can cause erosion of land, especially land with no plants to hold the dirt together with their roots.

continued

Erosion continued

EXPANSION:

If possible during outside time, find a rise in the landscape that is covered with grass or other vegetation. Ask the children what will happen to this area if water is poured on it. Using the child-size watering can, pour water on the incline with vegetation and discuss the results, noting that plants help to avoid soil erosion.

GROUP SIZE:

2–3 children

Evaporation

ADULT PREPARATION:

1. Number the cups 1–3 with a permanent marker.
2. Pour water in each cup, filling them to 1" from the top.

PROCEDURES:

1. Wearing smocks, children will add food coloring or liquid watercolor to each cup.
2. With adult assistance, children will measure the height of the water from the bottom of each cup, with a ruler.
3. Children will mark the water level with a permanent marker, with adult help.
4. Adult or older child will write measurements on Evaporation Experiment chart (on the next page).
5. If the weather is warm, one cup will be set near a window. In cool weather, the first cup will be set near a source of heat.
6. Second cup is set in the refrigerator.
7. Children decide where they would like to put the third cup.
8. Each week, children measure the height of the water from the bottom of each cup, and measurements are written on the chart.
9. Each week the children are asked, "Which cup lost the most water through evaporation? Which cup lost the least water through evaporation? Did any cups lose the same amount of water through evaporation?"

Notes: The cup sitting near the window or heat source will lose the most water through evaporation, because water evaporates more in heat and dry air. The cup in the refrigerator, where it is cool and moist, will lose very little water through evaporation.

ACTIVITY SUGGESTION:

For younger children, you may want to skip the measurement with a ruler. Instead, set the cups side by side each day and do a visual comparison.

GROUP SIZE:

3–4 children

continued

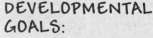

AGES: 3–5

DEVELOPMENTAL GOALS:

✄ To observe objects using the senses

✄ To understand and accept delayed gratification

LEARNING OBJECTIVE:

Using food coloring, water, cups, marker, ruler, and measurement sheet, the child will observe and measure evaporation.

MATERIALS:

Food coloring or liquid watercolor
Water
3 cups (must be identical in size and shape)
Permanent marker
Ruler
Smocks

Evaporation continued

	Evaporation Experiment Water Level		
	Cup 1	Cup 2	Cup 3
Week 1			
Week 2			
Week 3			
Week 4			

Which cup lost the most water through evaporation?

Which cup lost the least water through evaporation?

Did any cups lose the same amount of water through evaporation?

42

Expansion

AGES: 2–5

DEVELOPMENTAL GOALS:

- ✂ To observe liquid changing into a solid
- ✂ To increase self-help skills

LEARNING OBJECTIVE:

Using gallon milk jugs, water, cups, funnels, and a freezer, the children will observe the change in water as it freezes.

MATERIALS:

Two plastic gallon milk jugs with screw-on lids
Large container
Water
Small cups
Two funnels
Freezer
Towels

ADULT PREPARATION:

1. Rinse plastic gallon milk jugs.
2. Fill a large container with water.
3. Cover a table with towels.
4. Set milk jugs, water, and small cups on the table.
5. Place a funnel in each milk jug.

PROCEDURES (DAY 1):

1. Children may take turns dipping cups into the water and pouring water into milk jugs, using the funnel to fill both jugs to the top with water.
2. Adult screws lids on the milk jugs.
3. Ask the children, "What will happen if we put one of the jugs of water in the freezer?"

continued

Expansion continued

4. Put one jug in the freezer. Let it remain in the freezer for at least 24 hours.

5. Leave the other jug on the counter.

PROCEDURES (DAY 2):

1. Remove the jug from the freezer.

2. Set the two jugs side by side.

3. Ask, "What is different about these jugs?"

4. The jug left at room temperature will not show any change, but the jug put into the freezer will have swollen out of shape. (Water expands as it freezes.)

GROUP SIZE:

2–10 children

Feely Sock

ADULT PREPARATION:

1. Place one small classroom object into each sock.
2. Loosely knot the end of each sock.
3. Lay the filled socks on the table.

PROCEDURES:

1. Children take turns feeling the outside of the socks and feeling the shapes of objects in the socks.
2. Children attempt to identify the objects.
3. Once children have had a chance to identify the objects, unknot the socks.
4. Children pull the objects out of the socks to see if they were correct.
5. The objects are then returned to the socks, which are loosely knotted again.
6. Children may take another turn or allow another group of children to participate.

GROUP SIZE:

2–4 children

AGES: 2–5

DEVELOPMENTAL GOALS:

✂ To distinguish between objects by texture
✂ To improve problem-solving abilities

LEARNING OBJECTIVE:

Using socks and small objects, the child will identify objects by touch.

MATERIALS:

Large cotton or acrylic socks—adult size
Small objects from the classroom to fit inside socks (crayons, blocks, etc.)

F

Fishing

AGES: 2–5

DEVELOPMENTAL GOALS:

✂ To observe magnetic properties

✂ To coordinate large and small muscles

LEARNING OBJECTIVE:

Using sticks, string, magnetic wands, and paper fish hot-glued to tin can lids, the child will pretend to catch fish.

MATERIALS:

Small stick or wooden dowel
Smooth-edge can opener
Tin cans
Construction paper
Scissors
Fish stencil
Hot glue gun
String
Magnetic wand
Bucket or container
Paper clips (optional)

ADULT PREPARATION:

1. Using a smooth-edge can opener, take the lids off tin cans.
2. Wash and dry the lids.
3. Using a fish pattern, trace and cut out several fish, from construction paper.
4. Hot-glue a tin can lid to each fish. (If you do not have a smooth-edge can opener, fasten a large paper clip to each fish instead.)
5. Tie one end of a string to a small stick.
6. Tie the other end to a magnetic wand.
7. Lay the fish on the ground.

continued

Fishing continued

PROCEDURES:

1. Using the magnetic fishing pole, children will take turns "catching" the fish.
2. "Release" the fish that are caught into an empty bucket or container.
3. Continue until all the fish are caught.

GROUP SIZE:

2–3 children

Flashlight

AGES: 1–5

DEVELOPMENTAL GOALS:

- ✂ To recognize a shadow
- ✂ To visually identify shapes

LEARNING OBJECTIVE:

Using a flashlight, small stencils, and a darkened room, the child will identify shadows.

MATERIALS:

Large flashlight
Stencils of various shapes, in small sizes
Black construction paper
Scissors
Tape

ADULT PREPARATION:

1. Using stencils as guides, trace small shapes and cut them out of black construction paper.
2. Each shape must fit across the lens of the flashlight.

PROCEDURES:

1. After child turns on the flashlight, turn off the classroom lights.
2. Child will hold the flashlight 1–3 feet from the wall.
3. Ask child to notice how the flashlight makes a circle where it shines on the wall.
4. Turn the classroom lights back on and the flashlight off.
5. Show the child the shapes cut from construction paper.
6. Ask the child, "What would happen to the light if we taped one of these shapes on the flashlight?"
7. Allow the child to pick a shape.

continued

Flashlight continued

8. Tape that shape to the lens of the flashlight in a manner that does not show the tape (which would distort the shape of the shadow).

9. Turn the flashlight on and the classroom lights off.

10. Child holds the flashlight 1–3 feet from the wall, showing that the closer the flashlight is to the wall, the more distinct the shape becomes.

11. Ask the child what shape is the shadow made by the flashlight shining around the construction paper silhouette.

Notes: The stencil will block out all light except the part of the paper that is cut out. It will reflect the shape of the stencil on the wall.

If a lighter color paper or thinner paper is used, light will filter through the paper, making the shape indistinguishable. But black construction paper blocks out all light.

GROUP SIZE:

1–10 children

Float or Sink

DEVELOPMENTAL GOALS:

- ✂ To recognize similarities between objects
- ✂ To enhance cognitive development

LEARNING OBJECTIVE:

Using water and various objects, the children will discover whether objects float or sink.

MATERIALS:

Sensory table or large container
Water
Items that float (apple, cork, wood, pencil, plastic object, etc.)
Items that sink (screw, metal paper clip, key, spoon, etc.)

ADULT PREPARATION:

1. Fill sensory table or large container two-thirds full of water.

PROCEDURES:

1. Ask children to place items in the water one at a time, to see if they float or sink.
2. Ask the children, "What is the same about the things that float?"
3. Ask the children, "What is the same about the things that sink?"
4. Listen to the children's responses, guiding their answers if necessary.
5. Older children may write the names of the items that sink and float on the Sink or Float Experiment chart. Younger children may glue pictures of the items in the appropriate columns.

Notes: You can copy and cut out the pictures provided with the chart or cut them out of magazines or school supply catalogs. A digital camera may be used to create other pictures of items that float or sink.

GROUP SIZE:

2–3 children

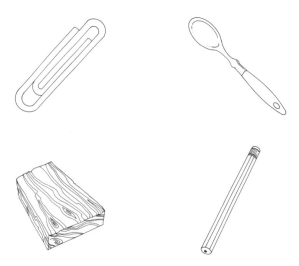

continued

Float or Sink continued

Float or Sink Experiment	
Float	Sink

F

DEVELOPMENTAL GOALS:

✂ To recognize colors

✂ To practice making predictions

LEARNING OBJECTIVE:

Using water and crayons, the children will discover whether different colors float or sink.

MATERIALS:

Sensory table or large container
Water
Different brands of crayons

Floating Crayons

ADULT PREPARATION:

1. Make a copy of the Floating Crayon Experiment chart for each child.
2. Fill the sensory table or large container two-thirds full of water.
3. Place crayons on the table.

PROCEDURES:

The children will complete the following steps:

1. Identify colors of crayons on the table.
2. Drop a crayon in the water to see whether it sinks or floats when asked, "What colors will float?" and "What colors will sink?"
3. Record results on the Floating Crayon Experiment chart by using that crayon to color the box under "Color" and the box under "Sink" in the first row if the crayon sank, or the box under "Color" and the box under "Float" if the crayon floated.
4. Repeat with the second crayon.

Notes: There are differences between the different brands of crayons. The same color of crayon from one brand may float, while the identical color of another brand may sink.

Whether a crayon floats or sinks is due to the amount of wax and the types of pigments used.

GROUP SIZE:

2–3 children

continued

Floating Crayons continued

Floating Crayon Experiment		
Color	Float	Sink

53

F

AGES: 3–5

DEVELOPMENTAL GOALS:

✂ To enhance counting skills

✂ To stimulate cognitive development

LEARNING OBJECTIVE:

Using a jar, water, a raw egg, measuring spoon, and salt, the child will determine how much salt is needed to make an egg float.

MATERIALS:

Plastic jar
Water
Raw egg
Measuring spoon
(teaspoon)
Bowl
Salt

Floating Egg

ADULT PREPARATION:

1. Place water in jar, filling it three-fourths full.
2. Put salt in bowl.

PROCEDURES:

1. Child places the egg carefully in the jar, gently guiding it to the bottom of the jar.
2. Child adds a spoonful of salt to the water and stirs.
3. Ask, "Did anything happen to the egg?"
4. Children take turns repeating step 2 until the egg floats, counting the spoonfuls of salt added.
5. When the egg floats, ask the children, "How many spoonfuls of salt did it take to make the egg float?"

continued

Floating Egg continued

Note: Salt water is more dense than fresh water. When salt was added to the water, the water became more dense than the egg. Therefore, the egg rose in the water.

 ## SAFETY PRECAUTION:

Wash hands after handling eggs.

GROUP SIZE:

2–4 children

F

DEVELOPMENTAL GOALS:

- ✂ To participate in a group project
- ✂ To observe objects using the senses

LEARNING OBJECTIVE:

Using two pieces of wood, the child will use friction to create heat.

MATERIALS:

Two pieces of smooth wood

Friction

ADULT PREPARATION:

1. Find two similar pieces of wood that are smooth and unfinished.

PROCEDURES:

1. Ask the children to feel the wood: "Does it feel cold, warm, or hot?"
2. The children may take turns rubbing the two pieces of wood together for as long as their attention span allows.
3. Once everyone has had a turn, ask the children to feel the wood again. Ask, "How does the wood feel now?"
4. Explain that the wood is warmer now because everyone has taken turns rubbing the wood together, and friction creates heat.

EXPANSION:

1. Ask the children to place both hands on their faces.
2. Ask, "How do your hands feel: cool, warm, or hot?"
3. Have them rub their hands together for as long as their attention span allows.
4. Ask the children to place their hands on their faces again and ask, "How do your hands feel now?"

GROUP SIZE:

6–10 children

56

Gak

DEVELOPMENTAL GOALS:

- ✄ To use sensorimotor skills
- ✄ To develop measurement skills

LEARNING OBJECTIVE:

Using borax solution and glue, the child will create gak.

MATERIALS:

Borax (purchased in the laundry aisle)
Water
Measuring cup
Bowl
Spoons
Small plastic cups
Food coloring or liquid watercolor
White school glue
Resealable plastic bags
Smock

ADULT PREPARATION:

1. Mix ¼ cup of borax with 4 cups of warm water.
2. Stir until the borax is dissolved.
3. Put white school glue in small bowl.

PROCEDURES:

The child will complete the following steps:

1. Wearing a smock, measure and mix 2 tablespoons of the borax mixture with 2 tablespoons of white school glue.
2. Add a couple of drops of food coloring or liquid watercolor.
3. Stir mixture well, with adult help if needed, for at least 2–3 minutes.
4. Watch as adult pours off the excess solution and rinses with water.
5. Roll, stretch, and bounce the gak that he or she has created.

Note: Store gak in a resealable plastic bag.

GROUP SIZE:

1–2 children

Germinating Grass Seeds

DEVELOPMENTAL GOALS:

- ✄ To increase awareness of nature
- ✄ To develop observation skills

LEARNING OBJECTIVE:

Using a sponge, grass seeds, water, and a plate, the child will observe grass growing.

MATERIALS:

Sponges
Scissors
Grass seeds
Water
Bowl
Small foam plates
Permanent marker
Source of sunlight

ADULT PREPARATION:

1. Put water in a bowl.
2. Cut sponges into smaller pieces.
3. Write children's names on rims of individual plates with the permanent marker.

PROCEDURES:

The child will complete the following steps:

1. Dip sponge in the bowl of water.
2. Place sponge flat on a plate.
3. Sprinkle grass seeds on top of sponge.
4. Check sponge daily, keeping it moist by adding water to the plate as necessary. (Water should not be poured directly onto the sponge.)
5. Observe grass growing from the seeds when they begin to germinate (within one to two weeks).

Note: Birdseed and radish seeds have been successfully used in place of grass seed.

GROUP SIZE:

2–4 children

Germs

AGES: 2–5

DEVELOPMENTAL GOALS:

✂ To observe reactions between objects

✂ To understand the importance of washing hands

LEARNING OBJECTIVE:

Using pepper, dish soap, and water, the child will observe soap dispersing pepper.

MATERIALS:

Pie plate
Water
Pepper
Dish soap

ADULT PREPARATION:

1. Fill pie plate two-thirds full of water.

PROCEDURES:

1. Have the child sprinkle pepper on top of the water.
2. Place a drop of dish soap on the child's finger.
3. Have the child place the soapy finger in the center of the pepper and watch as the pepper flies away from the soapy finger.

Notes: The soap spreads through the water moving the pepper. Relate this to the importance of washing hands with soap by saying that germs are like the pepper and fly away from soap.

GROUP SIZE:

1 child

Gravity

DEVELOPMENTAL GOALS:

- ✂ To recognize that objects have different weights
- ✂ To understand the effects of gravity

LEARNING OBJECTIVE:

Using a balancing scale, rock, penny, crayon, block, tissue, cotton ball, and crumpled paper, the child will weigh objects and demonstrate gravity's effects.

MATERIALS:

Rock
Penny
Crayon
Block
Tissue, crumpled
Cotton ball
Piece of paper crumpled into a ball
Balancing scale

ADULT PREPARATION:

1. Lay all objects on the table.

PROCEDURES:

1. Ask child to identify objects on the table.
2. Ask child to determine which object is the heaviest and which is the lightest, using balancing scale.
3. Help child sequence items from lightest to heaviest.
4. Ask the child, "If we were to drop these objects, which would fall fastest?"
5. Have the child pick up a light object and a heavy object and hold them at arms' length, then drop them simultaneously.
6. Ask, "Which object fell fastest?"

Notes: The objects should fall at the same rate; if they do not, it may be because they were not released at the same time. Try the experiment again, helping the child release the objects simultaneously. (Objects such as paper and tissue may create resistance when falling, so be sure the tissue and the paper are crumpled into a ball before dropping).

GROUP SIZE:

3–4 children

Hairy

AGES: 2½–5

DEVELOPMENTAL GOALS:

- ✄ To increase aware-ness of nature
- ✄ To demonstrate gardening skills

LEARNING OBJECTIVE:

Using a cup, potting soil, grass seed, spoon, permanent markers, pitcher, and water, the child will plant grass seeds.

MATERIALS:

Foam cup
Potting soil
Grass seeds
Spoon
Permanent markers
Smock
Child-size pitcher
Water

ADULT PREPARATION:

1. Write children's names on individual foam cups.
2. Under the child's name, write the cup's name, "Hairy."
3. Put water in a child-size pitcher.

PROCEDURES:

The child will complete the following steps:

1. While wearing smock, use permanent marker to draw a face on the cup.
2. Using a spoon, fill the cup two-thirds full of potting soil.
3. Sprinkle a spoonful of grass seeds on top of the soil.
4. Spoon ½" to 1" of soil on top of the seeds.
5. Water the soil, using child-size pitcher.
6. Place the cup near a source of sunlight.
7. Check cup daily to see if seeds have sprouted (within a week, the grass sprouts will start to grow) and report observations.

GROUP SIZE:

2–4 children

Hard or Soft

AGES: 2–5

DEVELOPMENTAL GOALS:

✄ To classify objects

✄ To expand vocabulary

LEARNING OBJECTIVE:

Using a rock, cotton, yarn, pan, socks, metal spatula, feathers, dough, and paper, the child will classify objects as either hard or soft.

MATERIALS:

Rock
Cotton ball
Skein of yarn
Pan
Socks
Metal spatula
Feathers
Dough
Two sheets of paper
Markers

ADULT PREPARATION:

1. Using a marker, write *soft* on one sheet of paper. Write *hard* on the other sheet of paper.
2. Lay both sheets of paper and all other items on the table.

PROCEDURES:

The child will complete the following steps:

1. Identify the items on the table.
2. Sort the items into two piles, placing soft items on the sheet of paper marked *soft* and hard items on the sheet of paper marked *hard*.

EXPANSION:

Children may cut, sort, and glue pictures of the items on the Hard or Soft Experiment chart in the appropriate columns as well as sorting the items into piles. But this is not a substitute for the hands-on exposure of the activity; be sure the children have an opportunity to touch and feel the items.

GROUP SIZE:

2–4 children

continued

Hard or Soft continued

Hard or Soft Experiment	
Hard	Soft

Heartbeat

AGES: 3–5

DEVELOPMENTAL GOALS:

- ✄ To promote familiarity with a stethoscope
- ✄ To recognize a heartbeat

LEARNING OBJECTIVE:

Using a stethoscope, children will listen to their hearts beating.

MATERIALS:

Stethoscopes
Cotton balls
Rubbing alcohol

ADULT PREPARATION:

1. Put rubbing alcohol on a cotton ball and clean the earpieces of the stethoscopes before use.

PROCEDURES:

1. Using stethoscopes, children will find and listen to their own heartbeats.
2. After listening to their own hearts beating, children will ask permission of other children to listen to their heartbeats.

Note: Children may need help finding their heartbeats.

⚠ SAFETY PRECAUTION:

With rubbing alcohol on a cotton ball, clean the earpieces of the stethoscope when each child is finished. Use a new cotton ball for each child.

GROUP SIZE:

1–2 children

Heat Transfer 1

ADULT PREPARATION:

1. Pour cold water in a child-size pitcher.
2. Pour hot water in one cup.

PROCEDURES:

The child will complete the following steps:

1. Pour cold water from pitcher into the other cup.
2. Place a metal spoon in each cup.
3. Count to 30 (with adult help).
4. Take spoons out of the water.
5. Feel the spoon that was in cold water.
6. Feel the spoon that was in warm water.
7. Respond when asked, "What is the difference in the spoons?"

Note: Explain that the heat in the hot water was transferred to the spoon.

GROUP SIZE:

1–4 children

AGES: 3–5

DEVELOPMENTAL GOALS:

- ✀ To observe similarities and differences
- ✀ To understand the concept of temperature

LEARNING OBJECTIVE:

Using cups, hot and cold water, metal spoons, and a pitcher, the child will demonstrate the transfer of heat.

MATERIALS:

Two cups
Hot water
Cold water
Child-size pitcher
Two metal spoons

Heat Transfer II

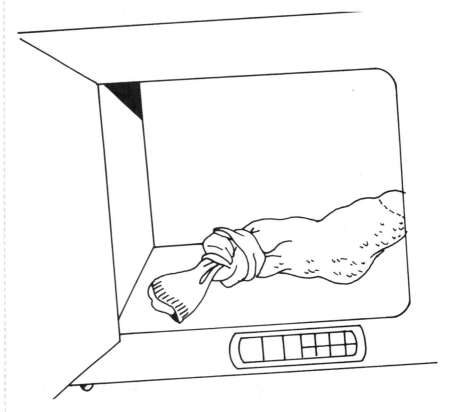

AGES: 2–5

DEVELOPMENTAL GOALS:

- ✄ To observe temperature changes
- ✄ To practice making predictions

LEARNING OBJECTIVE:

Using a sock, rice, measuring cup, and microwave, the child will heat rice, then transfer the heat from the rice to his or her body.

MATERIALS:

Adult-size cotton or acrylic socks
Large bowl
Uncooked regular rice (do not use instant rice)
Measuring cup
Microwave

ADULT PREPARATION:

1. Put rice in a large bowl.

PROCEDURES:

1. The child will measure 1–2 cups of regular rice.
2. The adult will hold the sock open as the child pours the rice into the sock, holding the sock over the bowl so any rice that spills will fall into the bowl.
3. The adult will tie a knot at the open end of the sock.
4. After asking, "What will happen if we put the sock in the microwave?" the adult will place the rice sock in the microwave for one minute.
5. The adult will remove the rice sock and allow the child to hold it or will place it on the back of the child's neck and ask, "How does the sock feel?"

continued

Heat Transfer II continued

Note: The heated rice sock will hold heat for 15–20 minutes.

⚠ SAFETY PRECAUTION:

Microwaves vary, so test the heat of the sock before giving it to the child.

GROUP SIZE:

2– 5 children

Heavy or Light

AGES: 4–5

DEVELOPMENTAL GOALS:

- ✂ To understand that objects have different weights
- ✂ To recognize numbers

LEARNING OBJECTIVE:

Using an ounce scale, paper, pencil, and objects of different weights, the child will measure objects and sequence them by weight.

MATERIALS:

Ounce scale
Paper cut into small pieces
Pencil
Various objects from the classroom or home (e.g., a block, bottle of glue, paintbrush, cup, dish)

ADULT PREPARATION:

1. Lay objects to be used on the table.

PROCEDURES:

1. Ask child to identify the objects on the table.
2. Ask child to weigh the first object, using the ounce scale, then write the weight of that object on a piece of paper and tape it to the object for the child.
3. Repeat with other objects.
4. Ask child to identify the number taped to each object, giving assistance as needed.
5. Ask child to sequence the items on the table, from lightest to heaviest.

GROUP SIZE:

3–4 children

68

Ice Trails

AGES: 2–5

DEVELOPMENTAL GOALS:

- ✂ To recognize colors
- ✂ To improve fine motor skills

LEARNING OBJECTIVE:

Using ice, nails, food coloring, salt, water, and eyedroppers, the child will create colored trails in ice.

MATERIALS:

Gallon-size coffee can or larger container
Water
Tray or pan
Nails
Food coloring or liquid watercolor
Salt
Small cups
Eyedroppers
Cup of warm water
Measuring cup
Smocks

ADULT PREPARATION:

1. Freeze water in coffee can or large container for at least 24 hours, until frozen solid.

2. Mix together ½ cup of salt and 1 cup of water in pan.

3. Heat water until the salt is dissolved.

4. Divide salt water into small cups.

5. Add food coloring or liquid watercolor to the cups, using a different color for each cup.

6. Remove the container of ice from the freezer and run water over the outside of the container, loosening the block of ice inside.

7. Remove the block of ice from the container and place it on a tray or in a pan.

8. Heat plain water and pour into another cup.

9. Place the cup of warm water, cups of colored salt water, and tray containing the block of ice on the table.

continued

Ice Trails continued

PROCEDURES:

The child will complete the following steps:

1. Wearing a smock, identify the colors of salt water in cups on the table.
2. Dip a nail into the cup of warm water.
3. Press the nail into the ice, making holes in the top of the ice block.
4. Using an eyedropper, put droplets of tinted salt water in the holes.
5. Watch as the salt melts the ice, allowing the color to spread into trails down through the block.
6. Check the ice trails throughout the day to monitor their progress.

Note: For young children who have difficulty using an eyedropper, put the tinted salt solution into small squeeze bottles.

GROUP SIZE:

2 children

Incline

DEVELOPMENTAL GOALS:

- ✂ To recognize similarities and differences
- ✂ To understand the concept of correlation

LEARNING OBJECTIVE:

Using toy cars and blocks, the child will demonstrate the effects of an incline.

MATERIALS:

Long rectangular blocks
Square blocks
Small, similar toy cars

ADULT PREPARATION:

1. Stack two square blocks on top of each other.
2. Lean a long rectangular block against the stack, creating an incline.
3. Make an identical incline beside it.
4. Check to be sure the toy cars will travel at the same speed when released simultaneously on the inclines. If not, find cars that will travel at the same speed.

PROCEDURES:

The child will complete the following steps:

1. Place a small car at the top of each incline.
2. Release the cars simultaneously.
3. Watch to see if the cars reach the bottom at the same time.
4. Try again if cars do not reach the bottom at the same time, being sure to release them simultaneously.

continued

Incline continued

5. Repeat the procedure, after the adult changes one incline by adding one or two blocks to its base (to make it higher than the other one).

6. When asked, report that the car on the steeper incline traveled faster, reaching the bottom first.

GROUP SIZE:

2 children

Jelly Beans

AGES: 2–5

DEVELOPMENTAL GOALS:

- ✂ To identify colors
- ✂ To observe transformations

LEARNING OBJECTIVE:

Using jelly beans, a clear carbonated beverage, a pitcher, and a cup, the child will observe a change in the color of the beverage.

MATERIALS:

Jelly beans
Small clear cups (one for each child)
Clear carbonated beverage
Child-size pitcher
Permanent marker
Masking tape

ADULT PREPARATION:

1. Label each cup with a child's name, writing directly on the cup if it is disposable and using masking tape if it is not.
2. Pour clear carbonated beverage into a child-size pitcher.

PROCEDURES (DAY 1):

1. Using the child-size pitcher, children will fill their cups one-third full of the clear carbonated beverage.
2. Each child will choose a jelly bean and identify the color.
3. Children will place jelly beans into their cups.
4. Adult will freeze the cups overnight.

continued

Jelly Beans continued

PROCEDURES (DAY 2):

1. Adult will remove the cups from the freezer and distribute them to the children.
2. Adult will pour clear carbonated beverage in a child-size pitcher.
3. Using the child-size pitcher, each child will add more clear carbonated beverage to his or her cup, filling it two-thirds full.
4. Children will observe that, as the frozen beverage in the bottom of each cup melts, it tints the liquid around it the same color as the jelly bean. (The drink will also taste like the jelly bean.)

Note: Some well-known brands of jelly beans will not work for this activity. Usually, the least expensive jelly beans work best.

SAFETY PRECAUTION:

If the ice in a cup melts completely, remove the jelly bean before allowing a child to drink the beverage.

GROUP SIZE:

2–4 children

Jet

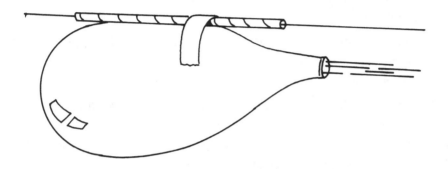

AGES: 2½–5

DEVELOPMENTAL GOALS:

✂ To understand air moves objects

✂ To interact with an adult

LEARNING OBJECTIVE:

Using a balloon, string, and straw, the child will observe air moving an object.

MATERIALS:

String or thin yarn
Masking tape
Balloons (do not use water balloons, which are too small)
Two straws
Scissors

ADULT PREPARATION:

1. Cut a length of string to reach from the ceiling to the floor.
2. Thread the string through a straw.
3. Tape one end of the string to the table.
4. Tape the other end of the string to the ceiling.
5. Cut a second length of string to run horizontally through the room.
6. Thread the second length of string through a straw.
7. Place two chairs several yards apart.
8. Tape one end of the string to each chair.
9. Make sure the vertical and horizontal strings are stretched tight.

continued

Jet continued

PROCEDURES:

The child will complete the following steps:
1. Watch as adult blows up a balloon, then take the balloon from the adult and hold the end firmly so air does not escape.
2. Hold balloon next to straw on vertical string while adult tapes balloon to the straw.
3. Let go of balloon when adult asks, "Let's see what happens when we let go of the balloon."
4. Watch as the balloon, attached to the straw, travels up the string.
5. Listen as adult explains the air in the balloon is like the air in jet engines which propells the plane.
6. Repeat steps 1–4, using the horizontal string and watching as the balloon releases air, propelling it along the string.

SAFETY PRECAUTION:

Supervise children closely; do not allow them to blow up balloons, which present a choking hazard.

GROUP SIZE:

1–2 children

Just Gelatin

ADULT PREPARATION:

1. Heat one cup of water in the microwave for 2–3 minutes.
2. Put powdered gelatin into a bowl.
3. Label two cups with each child's name.

PROCEDURES (DAY 1):

The child will complete the following steps:

1. Wash hands.
2. In a small cup, measure and mix 1 tablespoon gelatin with 4 tablespoons hot water and stir until gelatin is dissolved.
3. In another small cup, measure and mix 1 tablespoon gelatin with 2 tablespoons hot water and stir until gelatin is dissolved.
4. Put the cups on a tray and refrigerate overnight.

PROCEDURES (DAY 2):

The child will complete the following steps:

1. Wash hands.
2. After adult places gelatin cups on the table, remove gelatin from each cup with a spoon and place gelatin on plate.
3. Observe that the gelatin from the cup that contained less water is smaller in amount, very firm, and can be picked up with fingers, whereas the gelatin with more water added falls apart when picked up.
4. Eat the gelatin.

Note: The amounts of mix and water given are for use with regular gelatin. Amounts will change if a sugar-free mix is used.

 **SAFETY PRECAUTIONS:**

Maintain close supervision when children are working with hot water.

GROUP SIZE:

1–2 children

AGES: 3–5

DEVELOPMENTAL GOALS:

✂ To enhance fine motor skills
✂ To compare and contrast

LEARNING OBJECTIVE:

Using gelatin, water, cups, and spoons, the child will compare two methods of making gelatin.

MATERIALS:

Flavored gelatin (a 6-ounce box makes enough for 7 children; the box contains 14 tablespoons of dry mix)
Hot water
Bowl
Measuring spoons
Measuring cup
Small cups (two for each child)
Masking tape
Permanent marker
Tray
Plates (one for each child)
Spoons
Microwave

Kaleidoscope

AGES: 3–5

DEVELOPMENTAL GOALS:

- ✂ To develop fine motor skills
- ✂ To stimulate the use of the senses

LEARNING OBJECTIVE:

Using toilet tissue tube, resealable plastic bag, tissue paper, rubber band, markers, and crayons, the child will create a kaleidoscope.

MATERIALS:

Toilet tissue tube or paper towel roll (one for each child)

Sandwich size resealable plastic bag (one for each child)

Tissue paper (assorted colors)

Scissors

Rubber band (one for each child)

Markers

Crayons

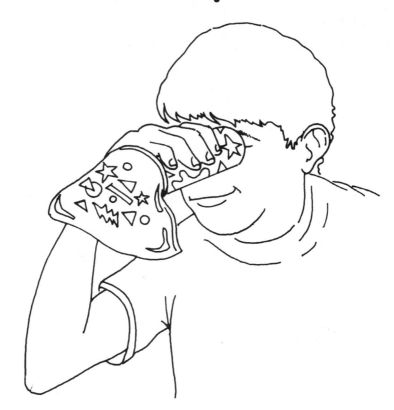

ADULT PREPARATION:

1. Place toilet tissue tube, markers, and crayons on the table.
2. Cut tissue paper into small pieces.

PROCEDURES:

The child will complete the following steps:

1. Decorate toilet tissue tube with marker and crayons.
2. Place colored tissue paper pieces in resealable plastic bag.
3. With adult help, seal the bag, leaving some air in the bag so the pieces of tissue paper can move around.
4. With adult help, place the sealed plastic bag against the end of the tube and watch as adult secures bag to the tube with a rubber band.
5. Hold kaleidoscope up to the light, rotating tube while looking through it so the tissue paper pieces will move around and produce different effects.

continued

Kaleidoscope continued

Note: Adding too much tissue will keep it from moving; it should move slowly when the tube is turned.

GROUP SIZE:

2–3 children

Kazoo

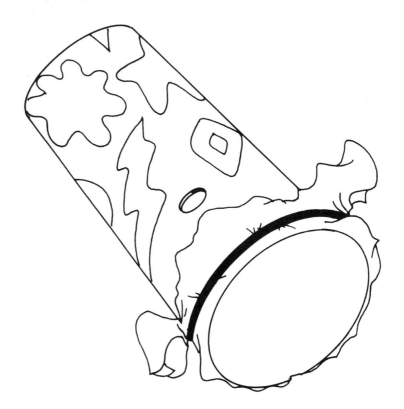

AGES: 4–5 (may be suitable for younger children if they have the ability to toot a song)

DEVELOPMENTAL GOALS:

- ✄ To stimulate the sense of hearing
- ✄ To delight in the joy of music

LEARNING OBJECTIVE:

Using toilet tissue tube, wax paper, markers, crayons, and a rubber band, the child will make a kazoo.

MATERIALS:

Toilet tissue tube (one for each child)
Wax paper
Markers
Crayons
Pencil or sharp scissors
Rubber band (one for each child)

ADULT PREPARATION:

1. Using a pencil or scissors, poke a hole approximately 1½" from the end of the tube.
2. Cut wax paper in a circle, approximately 2" wider than the diameter of the tissue tube opening.

PROCEDURES:

The child will complete the following steps:

1. Using markers and crayons, decorate toilet tissue tube.
2. With adult help, wrap wax paper circle around end of tube.
3. Watch as adult wraps rubber band around wax paper and tube, being careful not to cover up the hole.
4. Make tooting noises.

continued

Kazoo continued

5. Watch and listen as adult demonstrates how to toot a song by holding the open end of the tube over the mouth. The wax covered end is away from the body.

6. Duplicate what the adult has done by tooting into the open end of the tube.

GROUP SIZE:

2–4 children

Leaves

AGES: 2–5

DEVELOPMENTAL GOALS:

- ✄ To make comparisons
- ✄ To classify objects

LEARNING OBJECTIVE:

Using leaves and paper plates, the child will sort leaves.

MATERIALS:

Leaves
Paper plates

ADULT PREPARATION:

1. Send a note home asking children to bring in leaves, or take them on a nature walk to collect leaves.
2. Put one of each kind of leaf on a separate paper plate.

PROCEDURES:

1. Child will sort leaves by matching them to the original leaf on each plate.

EXPANSION:

Count and graph the types of leaves found.

ACTIVITY SUGGESTION:

If leaves in fall colors are used, have children sort them again according to color.

GROUP SIZE:

1–10 children

82

Lemon Juice Writing

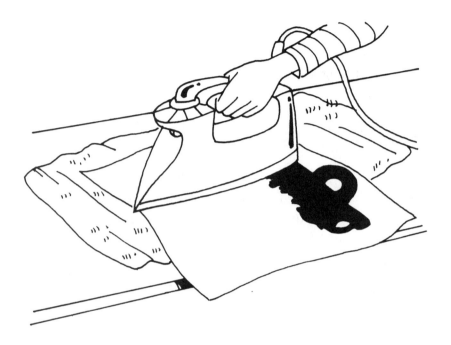

AGES: 3–5

DEVELOPMENTAL GOALS:

✂ To observe transformations

✂ To acquire prewriting skills

LEARNING OBJECTIVE:

Using lemon juice, cups, cotton swabs, white paper, and an iron, the child will write with lemon juice.

MATERIALS:

Lemon juice
Small cup
Cotton swabs
White paper
Towel
Iron

ADULT PREPARATION:

1. Place lemon juice in a small cup.
2. Place the cotton swabs, lemon juice, and paper on the table.

PROCEDURES:

The child will complete the following steps:

1. Dip a cotton swab in the lemon juice and write or draw on the paper.
2. Allow the paper to dry and observe that the lemon juice is invisible.
3. Place paper on a towel.
4. Watch as the adult irons the paper, and see the writing magically appear.

Note: Iron should be set on low. Children may iron the paper with one-on-one supervision.

GROUP SIZE:

3–4 children

L

DEVELOPMENTAL GOALS:

- ✄ To make comparisons
- ✄ To develop the sense of taste

LEARNING OBJECTIVE:

Using lemons, water, cups, sugar, measuring spoon, and a spoon, the child will compare ways of making lemonade.

MATERIALS:

Lemons
Knife to cut lemons
Cups (one for each child)
Child-size pitcher
Small bowl
Water
Sugar
Measuring spoon (½ teaspoon)
Spoons for stirring (one for each child)

Lemonade

ADULT PREPARATION:

1. Cut lemons into quarters.
2. Put water in child-size pitcher.
3. Put sugar in a small bowl.

PROCEDURES:

The child will complete the following steps:

1. Pour water into a cup, using child-size pitcher.
2. Squeeze a lemon quarter into the water and stir.
3. Taste the lemon and water mixture.
4. Measure and add ½ teaspoon of sugar to the liquid and stir.
5. Taste the mixture again and state whether it tastes better with or without the sugar.

GROUP SIZE:

2 children

84

Liquid Layers

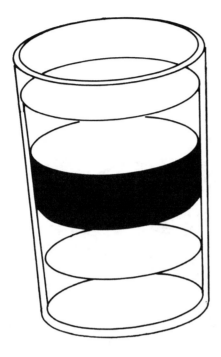

DEVELOPMENTAL GOALS:

- ✄ To improve eye-hand coordination
- ✄ To practice measuring

LEARNING OBJECTIVE:

Using a glass, pancake syrup, rubbing alcohol, oil, water, and a measuring cup, the child will make layers of liquid.

MATERIALS:

12-ounce clear glass
Pancake syrup (not low-calorie syrup, which is too watery)
Rubbing alcohol
Oil (vegetable)
Water
Blue food coloring
Four small plastic measuring cups with pouring spouts
Four child-size pitchers

ADULT PREPARATION:

1. Mix ¼ cup rubbing alcohol and blue food coloring in a small measuring cup with a pouring spout. Set aside.
2. Pour syrup in a child-size pitcher.
3. Pour oil in a child-size pitcher.
4. Put water in a child-size pitcher.

PROCEDURES:

The child will complete the following steps:

1. Measure and pour ¼ cup water into the glass.
2. Measure and add ¼ cup syrup.
3. Watch as adult adds the rubbing alcohol mixture.
4. Measure and add ¼ cup oil.
5. Observe that the liquids layer themselves in order of their density, with the most dense liquids on the bottom and the least dense liquids on top.

GROUP SIZE:

2 children

Liquid or Solid

AGES: 3–5

DEVELOPMENTAL GOALS:

- ✀ To observe transformations
- ✀ To improve social skills

LEARNING OBJECTIVE:

Using cornstarch, water, spoons, a large bowl, and a measuring cup, the child will mix a solution that is both liquid and solid.

MATERIALS:

Cornstarch
(16-ounce box)
Water
Large spoon
Spoon
Large bowl
Measuring cup
Child-size pitcher

ADULT PREPARATION:

1. Put water in a child-sized pitcher.

PROCEDURES:

1. Children take turns spooning cornstarch out of the box into a large bowl. Use the entire box.
2. Children slowly measure and add 1½ cups water (three children may add ½ cup each).
3. Using a large spoon, children take turns stirring well, as water is added.
4. Adult helps to thoroughly mix the ingredients.
5. Adult asks, "Is this a solid or a liquid?"

continued

Liquid or Solid continued

6. Children take turns poking the mixture with a finger, which doesn't yield and therefore appears to be a solid.

7. Children also take turns scooping up a spoonful of the mixture and holding it above the bowl, allowing it to run off the spoon and observing that it now appears to be a liquid.

EXPANSION:

Use this activity as a sensory experience. Have each child push a hand down into the mixture, then scoop the mixture up and allow it to run through the fingers. Add an additional ½ cup of water and mix with the hands. A milky liquid will remain on top, and the bottom will feel like silt.

GROUP SIZE:

3–4 children

Magnetic Bottle

AGES: 1–5

DEVELOPMENTAL GOALS:

- ✄ To observe magnetic properties
- ✄ To increase fine motor development

LEARNING OBJECTIVE:

Using a bottle, magnetic wand, and magnetic items, the child will move objects.

MATERIALS:

16- to 20-ounce plastic soda or water bottles
Magnetic wand
Magnetic marbles, paper clips, and other magnetic items that can be pulled by the wand

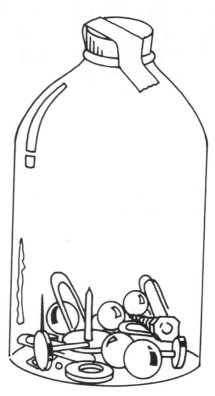

ADULT PREPARATION:

1. Rinse and air-dry the plastic soda or water bottles; keep the caps.
2. Remove the labels from the bottles.
3. Put magnetic balls, paper clips, and other small magnetic items in the bottles.
4. Put the caps on the bottles and tighten them; they may be glued or taped securely.

PROCEDURES:

1. Children will rub magnetic wands along the sides of the bottles, pulling the items up and down the bottle.

Note: This is ideal for younger children, because the small items are secure in the bottles.

GROUP SIZE:

1–5 children

Magnification

AGES: 2–5

DEVELOPMENTAL GOALS:

✂ To improve observation skills

✂ To recognize differences between objects

LEARNING OBJECTIVE:

Using magnifying glasses, colored water, wax paper, and eye-droppers, the child will observe droplets.

MATERIALS:

Different styles and types of magnifying glasses.
Small containers
Spoons
Water
Eyedroppers or small squeeze bottles
Food coloring or liquid watercolor
Waxed paper
Paper towels
Smocks

ADULT PREPARATION:

1. Mix water with coloring in small containers; stir with a spoon.
2. If the children are unable to use eyedroppers, put the colored solution in small squeeze bottles.
3. Put a sheet of waxed paper onto the table.

PROCEDURES:

1. Wearing smocks, children use eyedroppers or small squeeze bottles to squirt droplets of each color onto the wax paper.
2. Children examine the droplets with different magnifying glasses.
3. Adult asks, "Do the droplets look the same or different with each magnifying glass?"
4. Adult asks, "Do the droplets look the same or different sizes if you hold the magnifying glass close or farther away?"

GROUP SIZE:

2–3 children

Melted Crayons

AGES: 2–5

DEVELOPMENTAL GOALS:

- ✂ To observe transformations
- ✂ To classify objects

LEARNING OBJECTIVE:

Using warming tray, muffin cups, and crayons, the child will sort crayons and observe them melting.

MATERIALS:

Warming tray or electric skillet
Metal muffin pan or aluminum muffin liners
Broken pieces of crayons
Towels

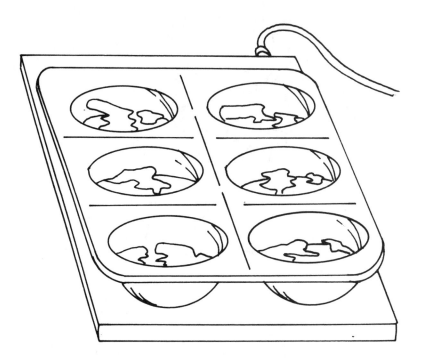

ADULT PREPARATION:

1. Collect broken pieces of crayons.
2. Remove all paper from crayons.
3. Surround warming tray or electric skillet with towels to protect child from the heat.

PROCEDURES:

1. Children will sort crayons by colors.
2. The children will place each separate color of crayon into a muffin cup.
3. The adult will place the muffin pan or aluminum liners onto warming tray.
4. If using an electric skillet, place on a medium setting until the crayons are melted.
5. The adult will remove the muffin pan or liners from the heat.
6. Once the melted crayons have cooled and hardened completely, remove them from the tins or liners and use them as round crayons.

continued

Melted Crayons continued

Note: Typical warming trays do not have various heat settings. If yours does, please follow the instructions for an electric skillet.

GROUP SIZE:

3–4 children

Mud

AGES: 2–5

DEVELOPMENTAL GOALS:

- ✂ To make comparisons
- ✂ To improve self-help skills

LEARNING OBJECTIVE:

Using cups, water, and soil, the child will create different compositions of mud.

MATERIALS:

3–4 small clear cups (for each group of children)
Soil
Water
Bowl
Spoons

ADULT PREPARATION:

1. Put water in a bowl.

PROCEDURES:

The child will complete the following steps:
1. Place equal amounts of soil in each cup.
2. Add 1 spoonful of water to the first cup and stir with a spoon.
3. Add 2 spoonfuls of water to the second cup and stir.
4. Add more spoonfuls of water to each additional cup. Count the spoonfuls added to each cup.
5. Answer the question, "What is the difference in the mud?" when asked.

Note: Do not use potting soil, which does not mix well with water. Use plain dirt.

GROUP SIZE:

3–4 children

Mystery Box

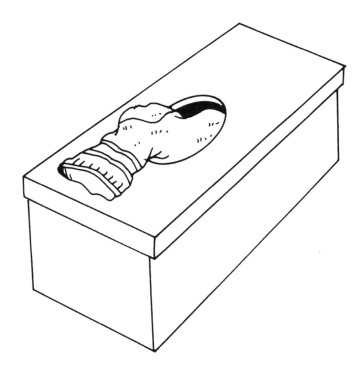

AGES: 2–5

DEVELOPMENTAL GOALS:

✄ To develop tactile discrimination skills

✄ To increase social development

LEARNING OBJECTIVE:

Using a box, sock, and items from nature, the child will identify objects through the sense of touch.

MATERIALS:

A large cotton or acrylic sock
Shoebox with a lid
Utility knife
Hot glue gun
Scissors
Small objects from nature to fit inside the sock (shell, nut, rock, leaf, twig, etc.)

ADULT PREPARATION:

1. Using the utility knife, cut a circle in the side of a shoebox. Cut the circle large enough for a hand to fit through.
2. Cut the foot off a cotton or acrylic sock.
3. Slip the sock into the hole of the shoebox.
4. Hot-glue the ends of the sock to the interior of the shoebox, with the rest of the sock extending outside the box.
5. Lay small nature objects (shell, nut, rock, leaf, twig, etc.) on the table.

PROCEDURES:

1. Ask children to identify the objects.
2. Put the objects in the shoebox and put the lid on the box.
3. Children take turns putting a hand into the sock and, then into the box, feeling an object, and identifying it.
4. Remove the lid from the box and see if all items were properly identified.

continued

Mystery Box continued

Note: Using a sock in the creation of the mystery box is optional, but use of the sock prevents the children from peeking into the hole and being able to identify the items visually.

 ### SAFETY PRECAUTION:

Use items large enough not to present a choking hazard

GROUP SIZE:

2–4 children

Nature Bracelet

AGES: 3–5

DEVELOPMENTAL GOALS:

✂ To increase aware-ness of nature

✂ To improve creativity

LEARNING OBJECTIVE:

Using contact paper and objects from nature, the child will create a bracelet.

MATERIALS:

Clear contact paper or wide masking tape
Small sea shells, leaves, acorns, grass, seeds, flower petals, or other objects from nature

ADULT PREPARATION:

1. Cut contact paper or wide masking tape into strips long enough to fit loosely around the child's wrist.

PROCEDURES:

1. Wrap the contact paper or masking tape loosely around children's wrists, sticky side up.

2. Supervise the children on a nature walk.

3. Help children choose nature items found outdoors and to stick them on their bracelets.

4. Assist the children in identifying the objects placed on their bracelets.

5. Cover the bracelet with clear contact paper to seal the items in the bracelet.

GROUP SIZE:

6–10 children

Nose Knows

AGES: 2–5

DEVELOPMENTAL GOALS:

✂ To stimulate the sense of smell

✂ To enhance eye-hand coordination

LEARNING OBJECTIVE:

Using cotton balls, film canisters, scents, and eyedroppers, the child will create and identify scented containers.

MATERIALS:

35 mm film canisters with lids (two for each child, plus one for each scent)

Cotton balls (one for each film canister)

Liquid flavoring (lemon, vanilla, strawberry, pineapple, etc.)

Small bowls

Eyedroppers or small squeeze bottles (one for each type of liquid flavoring)

Powdered spices (cinnamon, pepper, garlic, etc.)

Goggles

Child-size hammer

Roofing nail

ADULT PREPARATION:

1. Wearing goggles, use a hammer and nail to make a hole in the film canister lids.

2. Pour the liquid scents into separate small bowls.

3. Set a different eyedropper beside each scent. (If the children are unable to use eyedroppers, put the scent into small squeeze bottles.)

4. Make a canister of each scent by placing a cotton ball in separate film canisters. Add a different liquid flavoring or spice to each container. Put on the lids, which have been punctured with a nail.

5. Write the name of the scent on masking tape and put it on the bottom of the canister.

continued

Nose Knows continued

PROCEDURES:

The child will complete the following steps:

1. Place a cotton ball inside the film canister.
2. Choose a flavoring and put the scent on the cotton ball with an eyedropper or small squeeze bottle.
3. Put the lid on the canister, with adult assistance if necessary.
4. Watch as adult writes the name of the flavoring chosen on a small piece of masking tape.
5. Place the masking tape on the bottom of the film canister.
6. Place a cotton ball inside a second film canister.
7. Shake powdered spice onto that cotton ball.
8. Put the lid on the canister, with adult assistance if necessary.
9. Watch as adult writes the name of the spice on a small piece of masking tape.
10. Place the masking tape on the bottom of the film canister.
11. Smell the top of the canisters and identify the scents.
12. Smell the canisters the adult has made and attempt to find the same scents as the ones made.

GROUP SIZE:

3–4 children

Ocean in a Bottle

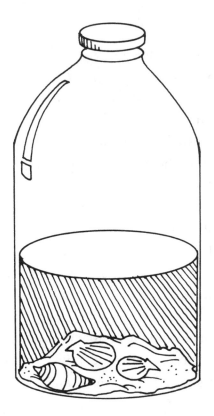

AGES: 3–5

DEVELOPMENTAL GOALS:

- ✂ To increase muscle development
- ✂ To improve observation skills

LEARNING OBJECTIVE:

Using a bottle, water, coloring, sand, funnel, spoon, pitcher, seashells, tablespoon, and eyedroppers, the child will create a miniature ocean.

MATERIALS:

16- to 20-ounce clear plastic water or soda bottles with caps
Water
Blue and green food coloring or liquid watercolors
Bowls
Sand
Funnel
Spoon
Child-size pitcher
Tiny seashells
Tablespoon
Eyedroppers or small squeeze bottles
Smocks

ADULT PREPARATION:

1. Put water in a child-size pitcher.
2. Put sand in a bowl.
3. Put blue and green food coloring or liquid watercolors in separate bowls.
4. Dilute each color with 2 tablespoons of water. (If children are unable to use eyedroppers, pour the solutions into small squeeze bottles.)

PROCEDURES:

The child will complete the following steps:

1. Wearing a smock, place a funnel in the mouth of the plastic bottle.
2. Fill the bottle two-thirds full of water, from the child-size pitcher.
3. Choose either blue or green coloring.

continued

Ocean in a Bottle continued

4. Add coloring to the bottle, using an eyedropper or small squeeze bottle.

5. Watch as adult puts the cap tightly on the bottle, then shake the bottle to mix the color.

6. Repeat steps 4–5 until the water in the bottle is the desired hue.

7. Watch as adult removes the cap and reinserts the funnel.

8. Add 4 tablespoons of sand.

9. Remove the funnel and add several small shells.

10. Watch as adult places cap tightly on the bottle.

11. Shake the bottle, creating a storm in the ocean when the sand and the shells are mixed with the water.

12. Set the bottle on the table or shelf and watch; when the storm calms, the sand and shells will separate from the water and settle on the bottom.

Note: Younger children would have difficulty making the ocean bottle, but would enjoy shaking the bottle and watching it settle.

GROUP SIZE:

2–3 children

Oil Spill

AGES: 3–5

DEVELOPMENTAL GOALS:

✂ To understand the effects of pollution

✂ To improve social skills

LEARNING OBJECTIVE:

Using water, oil, cotton ball, eyedropper, and a bowl, the child will attempt to clean water.

MATERIALS:

Container
Water
Oil (vegetable)
Two small bowls
Spoon
Cotton ball
Eyedropper
Small sponge

ADULT PREPARATION:

1. Fill a container two-thirds full of water.
2. Put vegetable oil in a small bowl.

PROCEDURES:

The child will complete the following steps:

1. Using a spoon, put a small amount of vegetable oil into the container with water.
2. When asked how the oil might be removed from the water, attempt to remove the oil with a cotton ball, eyedropper, or sponge.
3. Put liquid removed from the container into a small bowl.
4. Observe or feel the water to see if all the oil has been removed.

Note: This is a difficult task and may be linked to what happens when there is an oil spill in the ocean.

GROUP SIZE:

3–4 children

100

Packing Peanuts

DEVELOPMENTAL GOALS:

- ✂ To make comparisons
- ✂ To observe a transformation

LEARNING OBJECTIVE:

Using packing peanuts (biodegradable and regular) and water, the child will compare what happens when they are mixed with water.

MATERIALS:

Biodegradable packing peanuts
Regular packing peanuts
Cups
Water
Child-size pitcher

ADULT PREPARATION:

1. Pour water in child-size pitcher.
2. Put two clear cups on the table.

PROCEDURES:

The child will complete the following steps:

1. Place a biodegradable packing peanut in one cup.
2. Place a regular packing peanut in the other cup.
3. Pour water over each peanut from the child-size pitcher, until the peanuts are covered with water.
4. Observe that the regular peanut floats and is not changed by the water, but the biodegradable peanut begins to dissolve and mix with the water.
5. Listen as adult explains trash goes into landfills and takes up space, then respond when asked which type of peanut would be better for the landfill.

continued

Packing Peanuts continued

Notes: Packing peanuts may be collected from families, especially after the December holiday season. Biodegradable peanuts appear porous, whereas regular peanuts are usually smooth. Practice this experiment before using it with children to ensure that you have both types of packing peanuts.

GROUP SIZE:

2–4 children

Paleontologist

ADULT PREPARATION:

1. Clean chicken or turkey bones by removing all meat and gristle.
2. Put bones in a container.
3. Fill the container with ½ bleach and ½ water.
4. Allow bones to soak at least 24 hours.
5. Remove bones from bleach mixture and lay on newspaper to dry.
6. Fill sensory table or large container two-thirds full of cornmeal or sand.
7. Bury the sanitized bones in the cornmeal or sand.

PROCEDURES:

1. Explain to the children that a paleontologist digs for dinosaur bones.
2. Children sift through the cornmeal or sand, looking for bones.
3. Once the bones are found, children brush excess cornmeal or sand off the bones.
4. Children may hide the bones for other children to find.

GROUP SIZE:

2–4 children

AGES: 2–5

DEVELOPMENTAL GOALS:

- ✂ To increase fine motor control
- ✂ To role-play an adult occupation

LEARNING OBJECTIVE:

Using cornmeal, brushes, sifter, and bones, the child will enact the role of a paleontologist by sifting through "dirt" to find "fossils."

MATERIALS:

Sensory table or large container with lid
Cornmeal or sand
Various sizes of brushes
Kitchen sifter
Chicken or turkey bones
Container to soak bones
Bleach
Newspaper

Parachute

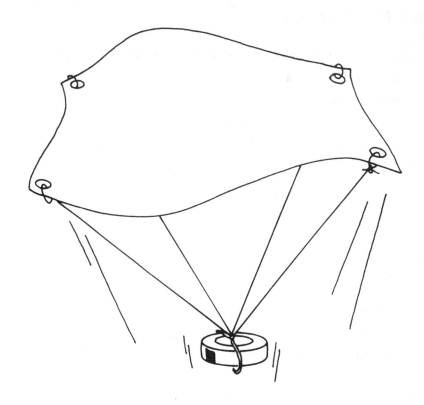

AGES: 4–5

DEVELOPMENTAL GOALS:

- ✂ To improve muscle development
- ✂ To observe resistance

LEARNING OBJECTIVE:

Using paper towel, string, pencil, and washer, the child will create a parachute.

MATERIALS:

Paper towel or light-weight plastic bag
String or heavy-duty thread
Pencil
Scissors
Large washer, small spool, little toy person, or other small object to use as a weight

ADULT PREPARATION:

1. Cut 12" square from paper towel or plastic bag.
2. Cut four pieces of string approximately 14" long.

PROCEDURES:

The child will complete the following steps:

1. Poke holes with pencil in each corner of 12" square, with adult help.
2. Tie one end of a piece of string through each corner hole in the square.
3. Watch as adult lays the square flat and ties all four strings in a knot.
4. Help tie washer or other weight to the knot.
5. Throw the parachute into the air and observe that it floats to the ground rather than falling quickly.

104

continued

Parachute continued

Note: Explain to children that the material creates resistance, slowing the parachute's descent.

GROUP SIZE:

2–5 children

Penny Cleaner

Ages: 3–5

DEVELOPMENTAL GOALS:

✂ To observe transformations

✂ To make comparisons

LEARNING OBJECTIVE:

Using pennies, water, salt, vinegar, bowls, and spoons, the child will clean pennies.

MATERIALS:

Dirty pennies (at least four per child)
Shiny new penny
4 clear cups
Water
Salt
Vinegar
Spoons
Child-size pitchers
Small bowl
Measuring spoons
Stirring spoon
Towel

ADULT PREPARATION:

1. Pour water and vinegar into separate child-size pitchers.
2. Put salt in a small bowl.
3. Set out four cups for each child.
4. Show the children a shiny new penny and an old, tarnished penny.
5. Ask, "What is the difference between the pennies?"
6. Ask, "What can we do to make the old penny look clean again?"

PROCEDURES:

Each child will complete the following steps:

1. Using a child-size pitcher, pour vinegar in two of the cups, filling each half full.
2. Pour water in the other two cups, filling each half full.
3. Measure and place a teaspoon of salt in one of the cups of water and one of the vinegar cups.

continued

Penny Cleaner continued

4. Add dirty pennies to each cup and stir.

5. Remove the pennies from the liquid, using a spoon, and put them on a towel.

6. Observe that the pennies from the vinegar and salt solution are cleanest.

Note: Explain that the vinegar mixed with salt is a cleaning agent; acting together, they cleaned the tarnish from the pennies.

SAFETY PRECAUTION:

Observe children closely, because pennies may present a choking hazard.

GROUP SIZE:

3–4 children

Pitch

DEVELOPMENTAL GOALS:

- ✄ To improve auditory discrimination
- ✄ To stimulate the sense of hearing

LEARNING OBJECTIVE:

Using glasses, water, metal spoons, and a pitcher, the child will create sounds.

MATERIALS:

3–5 identical glasses
Water
Metal spoons
Child-size pitcher

ADULT PREPARATION:

1. Pour varying amounts of water into identical glasses.
2. Put water in a child-sized pitcher.

PROCEDURES:

The child will complete the following steps:

1. Tap each glass gently with a spoon, noting that each makes a different sound.
2. Add more water to the glass most recently tapped, then tap again, noting the difference in sound after water is added.
3. Watch as adult pours enough water into two glasses to make their contents equal.
4. Gently tap these glasses, noting that now their sounds are the same.

Note: Identical glasses with equal amounts of water will sound the same. Glasses with more water will have a lower pitch. When the water takes up more space in a glass, the vibrations move more slowly. With less water the vibrations are able to move more rapidly, thus the higher the pitch.

GROUP SIZE:

2–5 children

Porcupine

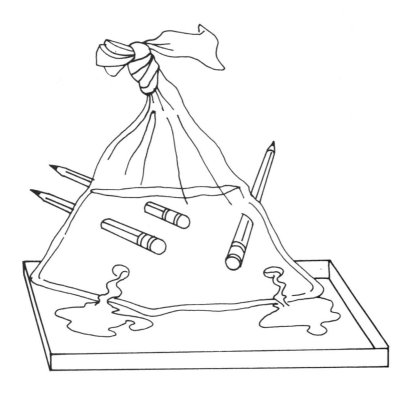

AGES: 3–5

DEVELOPMENTAL GOALS:

- ✄ To practice making predictions
- ✄ To increase fine muscle control

LEARNING OBJECTIVE:

Using skewers and a plastic bag of water, the child will create holes that do not leak.

MATERIALS:

Large container
Resealable plastic bags
Long wooden skewers or pencils
Water
Towels for cleanup

ADULT PREPARATION:

1. If pencils are being used, sharpen them until they have very pointed ends.
2. Fill a resealable plastic bag two-thirds full of water.
3. Seal the bag shut.

PROCEDURES:

1. Hold the bag of water (by its top) over a large empty container.
2. Ask, "What will happen if we poke holes through the bag?"
3. Have children take turns slowly pushing skewers or pencils through the bag, one at a time—in one side and out the other. (Skewers must be left sticking through the bag; they should not be removed.)
4. Point out that the bag does not leak water.
5. Ask the children, "What will happen if we pull the skewers out of the bag?"

continued

Porcupine continued

6. While still holding the bag over the large empty container, have the children take turns slowly pulling the skewers or pencils out of the bag and watch as the water springs out of the holes.

Note: When the skewers or pencils are in the bag they block the holes and prevent leakage; once the blockages are removed, the water will spring out of the bags.

GROUP SIZE:

2–4 children

Quiet or Loud

ADULT PREPARATION:

1. Place plastic animals or picture cards of animals on the table in random order.

PROCEDURES:

1. Ask the children to whisper their names. Explain that this is a quiet sound.

2. Next ask the children to shout their names. Explain that this is a loud noise.

3. Explain that some animals are quiet and some are loud.

4. Ask the children to identify the animals.

5. Ask the children to imitate the noises the animals make.

6. Ask the children to sort the animals into two sections, putting quiet animals on one side of the table and loud animals on the other side.

EXPANSION:

Lay out rhythm instruments. Ask the children to alternate between making loud noises and quiet noises.

GROUP SIZE:

2–4 children

AGES: 2–5

DEVELOPMENTAL GOALS:

✂ To understand object classification

✂ To develop auditory discrimination

LEARNING OBJECTIVE:

Using plastic animals or animal cards, the child will sort animals by the volume of sound that each makes.

MATERIALS:

Plastic animals or picture cards of quiet animals (e.g., mouse, rabbit, giraffe, snake, turtle, lizard)

Plastic animals or picture cards of noisy animals (e.g., lion, dog, owl, sheep, cow, rooster)

Quivering Quarters

AGES: 2–5

DEVELOPMENTAL GOALS:

✂ To improve observation skills

✂ To enhance eye-hand coordination

LEARNING OBJECTIVE:

Using a quarter, baking soda, vinegar, an eyedropper, and a plate, the child will make the quarter move.

MATERIALS:

Quarters
Small bowls
Eyedroppers or small squeeze bottles (one for each child)
Ceramic or plastic plate (one for each child)
Baking soda
Vinegar
Spoons

ADULT PREPARATION:

1. Pour baking soda into a small bowl.
2. Pour vinegar in a separate bowl.
3. If eyedroppers are too difficult for children to use, put the vinegar in small squeeze bottles.

PROCEDURES:

The child will complete the following steps:

1. Using an eyedropper, put a quarter-size amount of vinegar on plate.
2. Dip quarter in baking soda, lightly coating both sides of quarter.
3. Put the quarter into the vinegar on the plate and watch as the quarter shifts and moves.

Note: Explain to children that the baking soda and vinegar create a gas that forces the quarter to move.

GROUP SIZE:

2–4 children

Racing Colors

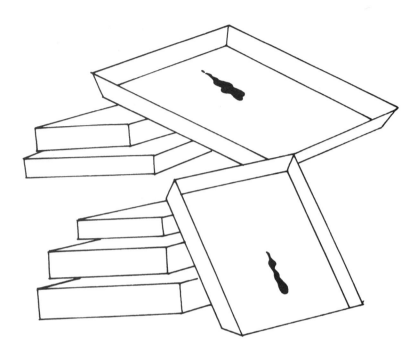

DEVELOPMENTAL GOALS:

- ✂ To make comparisons
- ✂ To observe the effects of inclines

LEARNING OBJECTIVE:

Using trays, blocks, colored water, and eyedroppers, the child will demonstrate the effects of inclines.

MATERIALS:

Aluminum cookie sheets, or trays covered with aluminum foil
Food coloring or liquid watercolor
Water
Small bowls
Eyedroppers or small squeeze bottles
Smocks
6–8 blocks
Large towels
Measuring spoons
Stirring spoon

ADULT PREPARATION:

1. Put 2 tablespoons of water into each small bowl or cup.
2. Using a spoon, stir in several drops of food coloring or liquid watercolor until desired hue is achieved. If children are unable to use eyedroppers, put the diluted coloring into small squeeze bottles.
3. Cover the table with a towel to absorb the colored water.

PROCEDURES:

The child will complete the following steps:

1. Stack two blocks on top of each other.
2. Lean an aluminum cookie sheet against the stacked blocks with adult assistance, creating an incline.
3. Make a second stack of blocks, using more than two blocks.
4. Lean another cookie sheet against it.

continued

Racing Colors continued

5. Using an eyedropper, place droplets of color on the top of each incline, trying to release the droplets simultaneously.

6. Observe that the droplets of color on the steeper incline move faster, reaching the bottom first (if the droplets were released simultaneously).

GROUP SIZE:

2–4 children

Rainbow

AGES: 2–5

DEVELOPMENTAL GOALS:

✂ To recognize colors

✂ To make predictions

LEARNING OBJECTIVE:

Using whole milk, food coloring, and dish detergent, the child will observe colors spreading.

MATERIALS:

Whole milk
Liquid dish detergent (Dawn® works best)
Clear glass pan such as a pie plate
Food coloring
Small squeeze bottles
Smocks

ADULT PREPARATION:

1. Put detergent in a small squeeze bottle.
2. Pour whole milk into clear pan, filling it one-fourth to one-half full.

PROCEDURES:

The child will complete the following steps:

1. Wearing a smock, place one drop of each color of food coloring in the milk, spacing colors around the bowl.
2. Identify the colors in the milk.
3. Using small squeeze bottle, place one drop of dish detergent on top of each drop of food coloring.
4. Watch the colors spread throughout the milk.

Note: The detergent breaks up the fat in the milk, causing it (and the coloring) to disperse.

GROUP SIZE:

2–5 children

® The Procter & Gamble Company. Used by Permission.

Rising Rice

AGES: 2–5

DEVELOPMENTAL GOALS:

✄ To improve observation skills

✄ To practice making predictions

LEARNING OBJECTIVE:

Using a glass, water, rice, vinegar, baking soda, a measuring spoon, and a stirring spoon, the child will observe the effects of mixing ingredients.

MATERIALS:

12-ounce glass (clear)
Water
Rice
Vinegar
Baking soda
Measuring spoon
Stirring spoon
Optional: magnifying glass
Bowls

ADULT PREPARATION:

1. Fill glass with water, leaving approximately a 1" space at the top.
2. Put rice in one bowl, baking soda in the second bowl, and vinegar in the third bowl.

PROCEDURES:

The child will complete the following steps:

1. Measure 1 tablespoon of rice and put it into the glass of water.
2. Observe that rice falls to the bottom of the glass.
3. Measure 1 teaspoon of baking soda, add it to the water, and stir with the spoon.
4. Observe that the rice remains at the bottom of the glass.
5. Measure and add 2 tablespoons of vinegar to the water mixture, stirring with the spoon.
6. Watch as the rice begins to rise and fall.

continued

Rising Rice continued

Notes: Explain to children that the mixture of vinegar and baking soda creates a gas. Tiny gas bubbles attach themselves to the grains of rice, and the rice rises with the bubbles, but then gravity forces the rice to fall. (Brown rice and instant rice may also be used, but the instant rice is lighter and floats on the top from the beginning, before the vinegar is added. A few minutes after adding the vinegar, however, it will began to move up and down.)

VARIATION:

Give the children a magnifying glass to enable them to closely observe the bubbles and rice moving.

GROUP SIZE:

2–4 children

Rough or Smooth

AGES: 2–5

DEVELOPMENTAL GOALS:

- ✂ To understand object classification
- ✂ To develop tactile discrimination

LEARNING OBJECTIVE:

Using rough and smooth items, the child will sort objects by texture.

MATERIALS:

Items that are rough (e.g., sandpaper, burlap, corrugated cardboard, emery board)

Items that are smooth (e.g., cotton ball, silk, aluminum foil, mirror)

ADULT PREPARATION:

1. Lay rough and smooth objects on the table in random order.

PROCEDURES:

The child will complete the following steps:

1. Identify the objects on the table.
2. Sort the objects according to whether they are rough or smooth, by placing smooth objects on one side of the table and rough objects on the other.

GROUP SIZE:

2–4 children

Running Colors

ADULT PREPARATION:

1. Put newspaper on the table.
2. Set coffee filter on the newspaper.
3. Fill a small bowl with water.
4. Set cotton balls on the table.

PROCEDURES:

1. Using the brown water based markers, the child will make a quarter sized circle in the middle of the filter. Fill the circle with the brown color. The adult may help if needed.
2. The child will dip a cotton ball in water.
3. Next the child sets the cotton ball on the brown circle in the filter.
4. The child may observe the filter periodically.
5. The brown color will spread throughout the filter separating into the different colors that make up brown.

Note: Brown is made up of all colors. When the water separates them, the colors spread around the edges of the coffee filter.

GROUP SIZE:

2–4 children

AGES: 2–5

DEVELOPMENTAL GOALS:

- ✂ To identify colors
- ✂ To observe the colors that create brown

LEARNING OBJECTIVE:

Using brown markers, coffee filters, cotton balls, water, and newspaper, the child will observe color spreading.

MATERIALS:

Brown water based markers
Large coffee filters (one for each child)
Cotton balls
Small bowl of water
Newspaper

Screeching Bird

AGES: 3–5

DEVELOPMENTAL GOALS:

✂ To develop the sense of hearing

✂ To increase creativity

LEARNING OBJECTIVE:

Using plastic cups, sponges, construction paper, string, glue, paper clip, and a bowl of water, the child will create a screeching bird.

MATERIALS:

Plastic cups (one for each child)
Sponges
Construction paper
Scissors
String
Nail
White school glue
Feathers (available at craft stores)
Paper clips
Small bowls (Day 2)
Water (Day 2)

ADULT PREPARATION:

1. Cut bird's eyes, beak, and wattle out of construction paper.
2. Cut sponges into ½" by ¾" rectangles. Make one for each child.
3. Use a nail to poke a hole in the bottom of the cup.
4. Cut the string into 12" lengths.

PROCEDURES (DAY 1):

The child will complete the following steps:

1. Help adult tie one end of string to paper clip.
2. Push other end of string through the hole in the bottom of the cup.
3. Pull string through the cup so paper clip rests against outside of cup bottom.
4. Help adult tie the other end of string to the small sponge rectangle.
5. Place cup upside down on the table.

continued

Screeching Bird continued

6. Tuck string inside the cup (to avoid getting glue on the string).
7. Glue feathers to the cup bottom, with cup sitting upside down and feathers sticking up.
8. Glue beak, eyes, and wattle to the cup, making a bird.
9. Let glue dry overnight.

PROCEDURES (DAY 2):

After adult places small bowl of water and the child's bird on the table, the child will complete the following steps:

1. Dip sponge rectangle into the water and squeeze out the excess.
2. Hold the cup with one hand. With the other hand, hold the sponge between thumb and forefinger, pinch top of the string with the sponge.
3. Quickly move sponge down the string to make a screeching noise.

GROUP SIZE:

3 children

Seeds 1

DEVELOPMENTAL GOALS:

✂ To introduce gardening techniques

✂ To observe plants grow

LEARNING OBJECTIVE:

Using seeds, cups, soil, a spoon, a pitcher of water, and a growth chart, the child will plot the growth of a plant.

MATERIALS:

Three or four different kinds of seeds

Small cups (one per child for each kind of seed)

Potting soil

Large spoon for potting soil

Tape

Toothpicks

Child-size pitcher with water

Scissors

ADULT PREPARATION:

1. Photocopy each seed package, reducing the image to make a marking flag.
2. Cut out the copies and tape each one to a toothpick, making one of each kind for each child.
3. Glue another copy of each seed package in the first column of the seed growth chart, making a chart for each child.
4. Put water in a child-sized pitcher.

PROCEDURES:

The child will complete the following steps:

1. Fill each cup one-half to three-fourths full of potting soil.
2. Use a finger to make a hole in the dirt in each cup.
3. Bury a seed in each hole, putting a different type of seed in each cup, and identify it with that seed's marking flag.

continued

122

Seeds 1 continued

4. Using child-size pitcher, water the seeds.
5. Check and graph seed growth chart daily, drawing (in each box on the chart) the amount of plant growth above the dirt.

GROUP SIZE:

3–4 children

Seed Growth Chart							
	Day 1	Day 2	Day 3	Day 4	Day 5	Day 6	Day 7

Seeds II

AGES: 2–5

DEVELOPMENTAL GOALS:

✂ To classify objects by matching

✂ To identify plants

LEARNING OBJECTIVE:

Using a seed chart and seeds, the child will identify and match seeds.

MATERIALS:

Two poster boards
Seed packets
    (two of each)
Glue
Clear tape
Marker
Scissors
Hook and loop tape or
    masking tape

ADULT PREPARATION:

1. Glue one of each type of seed package on the first piece of poster board, creating a seed poster.
2. Glue some seeds of that type under each package on the poster.
3. Write the name of each type of seed underneath the package and seeds.
4. Cut the remaining piece of poster board into pieces of equal size, to make seed cards.
5. Glue one seed package and some of that type of seed on each seed card, also writing the seed's name on the card.
6. Use wide clear tape to cover and secure seeds on the poster and on the cards.
7. Attach a piece of hook and loop tape above each seed package on the poster.
8. Attach an opposing piece of hook and loop tape to the top back of each seed card.
9. Lay seed cards on the table.
10. Lay the seed poster on the table or prop it against a wall.

PROCEDURES:

The child will complete the following steps:
1. Identify the plant on each seed package.
2. Match the seed cards to the poster board.
3. Attach the cards to the poster board with the hook and loop tape.

Notes: Use seeds of plants that are familiar to the children. Limit the number of seeds to match, depending on the children's age and attention span.

GROUP SIZE:

2–3 children

124

Soil Mix

AGES: 2–5

DEVELOPMENTAL GOALS:

- ✄ To make predictions
- ✄ To increase observation skills

LEARNING OBJECTIVE:

Using potting soil, plain dirt, water, cups, spoons, plates, measuring cups, and a magnifying glass, the child will mix two types of soil with water and observe the results.

MATERIALS:

Potting soil
Plain dirt from outdoors
Water
Large, clear cups
Spoons
Small clear or white plates
Measuring cup
Magnifying glass

ADULT PREPARATION:

1. Take samples of dirt from outside. If possible, find two different types or colors of soil.
2. Put ½ cup of potting soil and ½ cup of each type of dirt into separate cups.

PROCEDURES:

The child will complete the following steps:

1. Measure and add 2 cups of water to each cup, then stir with a spoon.
2. Observe that the plain dirt mixes with the water, dissolving almost completely.
3. Observe that the potting soil doesn't mix well with the water.
4. Put a spoonful of each mixture on a separate plate.
5. Examine the mixtures with a magnifying glass, noting that the water containing potting soil is still clear, but the water with plain dirt in it is now the color of the dirt.

continued

Soil Mix continued

Note: Some areas of the country have a lot of clay in the soil. The clay and water mix extremely well, and the water will reflect the color of the clay.

EXPANSION:

Leave the cups sitting undisturbed for a day or two, and the soil or dirt and water will eventually separate, leaving the water clear. The plain dirt will sift to the bottom of its cup. Lighter particles found in potting soil and debris from the soil will float on top of the water, and heavier particles will fall to the bottom.

GROUP SIZE:

2–4 children

Static Electricity

AGES: 3–5

DEVELOPMENTAL GOALS:

- ✄ To observe the effects of static electricity
- ✄ To interact with an adult

LEARNING OBJECTIVE:

Using a balloon and an aluminum soda can, the child will observe the effects of static electricity.

MATERIALS:

Balloon
Aluminum soda can

ADULT PREPARATION:

1. Blow up balloon and tie securely.
2. Empty and rinse aluminum soda can.

PROCEDURES:

The child will complete the following steps:

1. Put soda can on its side, on the floor or table.
2. Watch as adult rubs a balloon across his or her clothing or through hair.
3. Watch as adult places the balloon one to three inches above the can and then moves the balloon.
4. Observe the can as it attempts to follow the balloon.

continued

Static Electricity continued

Note: Explain that rubbing a balloon on hair or clothing creates static electricity, which attracts the aluminum can.

⚠ SAFETY PRECAUTION:

Adults handle the balloon due to the choking hazards involved with balloons.

GROUP SIZE:

3–10 children

Taste Test

DEVELOPMENTAL GOALS:

✂ To develop the sense of taste

✂ To identify common foods using only the sense of taste

LEARNING OBJECTIVE:

Using common foods and a blindfold, the child will identify foods.

MATERIALS:

Plates (one for each child)
Several fresh fruits and vegetables
Platter
Knife
Blindfold

ADULT PREPARATION:

1. Wash fruits and vegetables, then peel if necessary and cut into bite-size pieces.

2. Place food on a platter.

3. Put a small sample of each food on a plate.

PROCEDURES:

1. Use the blindfold to cover the child's eyes.

2. Place a piece of food in the child's hand.

3. Invite the child to feel the texture of the food and guess what it is.

4. Ask the child to taste the food and attempt to describe and identify it.

5. Repeat steps 2–4 with a different food.

6. Once all of the food has been tasted and identified, show the child another plate with identical samples of food.

7. Ask the child to identify each food and select food to taste that he or she was not able to identify in the taste test.

continued

Taste Test continued

Note: Some children will not want to wear a blindfold. These children may simply close their eyes or shield their eyes with their hands.

 **SAFETY PRECAUTION:**
Be aware of food allergies and make sure there are no choking hazards for young children.

GROUP SIZE:

2–10 children

Terrarium

AGES: 2–5

DEVELOPMENTAL GOALS:

- ✄ To introduce gardening techniques
- ✄ To observe plants growing

LEARNING OBJECTIVE:

Using a plastic jar, rocks, potting soil, plants, a scoop, pencil , and water in a watering can, the child will create a terrarium.

MATERIALS:

Plastic jar with wide mouth lid (one for each child)
Rocks or aquarium gravel
Potting soil
Small plants with roots intact
Scoop
Pencil
Child-size watering can
Water

ADULT PREPARATION:

1. Clean and remove the label of a wide mouthed plastic jar. Save the lid.
2. Put water in the child-size watering can.

PROCEDURES:

1. The child will place a layer of gravel on the bottom of the jar. The layer should be approximately 1" deep.
2. Using the scoop the child will place potting soil on top of the gravel.
3. The jar should be ¼ to ⅓ full of soil.
4. The child will poke a hole in the dirt with the pencil.
5. The child will place the roots of the plant in the hole. The stem needs to be partly in the soil.
6. The child will pat the soil around the stem to secure it.
7. If the mouth of the jar is too narrow for a hand to fit into, use the pencil to push the dirt.

continued

Terrarium continued

8. Repeat steps 4–7 to put more plants in the terrarium.
9. Using a watering can, the child will lightly water the plant.
10. The adult will put the lid on the jar.
11. The child will place the terrarium where it will receive sunlight.

GROUP SIZE:

1 child

Tie-Dyed Shirts

AGES: 2–5

DEVELOPMENTAL GOALS:

✂ To observe a transformation

✂ To increase creativity

LEARNING OBJECTIVE:

Using a T-shirt, fabric dye, squeeze bottles, newspapers, a fork, and plastic bag, the child will create a tie-dyed shirt.

MATERIALS:

Fabric dye
Small squeeze bottles
Water
White T-shirts
    (prewashed—one
    for each child)
Metal fork
Rubber bands
Newspaper
Plastic grocery bags
Masking tape
Permanent marker
Smocks

ADULT PREPARATION:

1. Ask families to send in prewashed white T-shirts.
2. Mix fabric dye with water according to package directions.
3. Pour dye into small squeeze bottles. Use one bottle for each color. It works best to have bottles with smaller openings so the dye doesn't run out too fast.
4. Write each child's name on the tag or inside collar of a T-shirt, with a permanent marker.

PROCEDURES:

1. Wearing a smock, place T-shirt in water.
2. With adult's help, squeeze out excess water.
3. Lay T-shirt flat on the table.
4. Put the prongs of a metal fork into the center of the T-shirt.
5. Turn the fork in a circular motion. (The shirt will wrap up in a circle.)

continued

Tie-Dyed Shirts continued

6. With adult assistance, stretch many rubber bands across the wound-up T-shirt, securing the T-shirt in a circle.

7. Lay the T-shirt on a pad of newspaper.

8. Using squeeze bottles, squirt the dye onto the shirt.

9. Turn the shirt over, putting different colors of dye on each side.

10. When finished, put the shirt in a plastic grocery bag and tie the bag shut. Write the child's name on the outside of the bag with a permanent marker.

Notes: The T-shirts must sit for 24 hours before being washed. You may send the T-shirts home with washing instructions or wash them if you have the facilities. T-shirts should be washed and rinsed in cold water, without detergent, separately from other laundry, and tumble-dried on low.

GROUP SIZE:

2–3 children

Tin Can Telephone

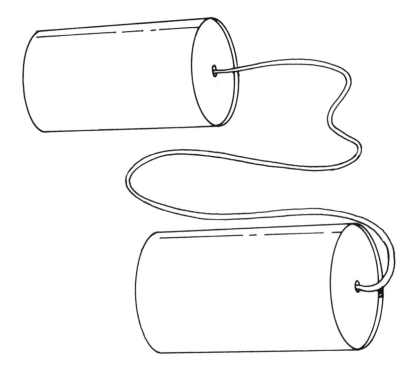

DEVELOPMENTAL GOALS:

✂ To make comparisons
✂ To improve auditory discrimination

LEARNING OBJECTIVE:

Using tins cans, foam cups, strings, and washers, the child will simulate using a telephone.

MATERIALS:

Smooth-edge can opener
Two empty tin cans (identical in shape and size)
Two foam cups
String (at least 20' long)
Washers
Child-size hammer
Nail
Scissors
Goggles

ADULT PREPARATION:

1. Cut the lid off one end of each tin can, using smooth-edge can opener.
2. Wash and dry the cans.
3. Use the nail to hammer a hole in the center of the remaining end of each can.
4. Thread one end of the string through the hole in the end of each can and knot a washer on the end of the string inside the can. The distance between the two cans when the string is stretched tight should be 6–10 feet.
5. Repeat steps 3–4 with foam cups.

PROCEDURES:

1. Allow two children to use the "telephone" at one time.
2. Children stand apart, each holding one can. The string should be stretched tight.

continued

Tin Can Telephone continued

3. Child 1 talks into the can while child 2 holds the can to one ear and listens.
4. Child 2 talks into the can and child 1 holds the can to one ear to listen.
5. Exchange the tin can telephones with the foam cup telephones.
6. Ask, "Is there any difference in the telephones?"

Note: If children have difficulty hearing through the can/cup, ask them to cover their other ear with their hand to block out background noise.

GROUP SIZE:

2 children

Tornado

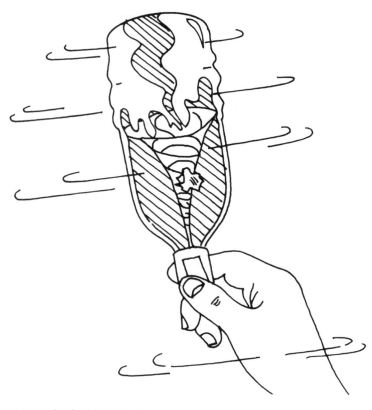

ADULT PREPARATION:

1. Empty and wash a soda bottle and its cap.
2. Remove the label on the bottle.
3. Write child's name on bottle with permanent marker.
4. Put water in the child-size pitcher.
5. Cut or tear small pieces of aluminum foil.
6. Put all supplies on the table.

PROCEDURES:

The child will complete the following steps:

1. Wearing a smock, place a funnel in the mouth of the bottle.
2. Fill the bottle three-fourths full of water, using the child-size pitcher.
3. Add yellow food coloring to the water.
4. Crumple a small piece of aluminum foil and drop it into the bottle.
5. Watch as adult tightens the cap on the bottle.

continued

T

DEVELOPMENTAL GOALS:

✄ To observe the circular movement of a tornado

✄ To improve muscular coordination

LEARNING OBJECTIVE:

Using a bottle, funnel, water, pitcher, food coloring, aluminum foil, and smock, the child will create a tornado.

MATERIALS:

16- to 20-ounce soda bottle with lid (one for each child)
Funnel
Water
Child-size pitcher
Yellow food coloring
Aluminum foil
Smocks
Permanent marker

Tornado continued

6. Turn the bottle upside down.
7. Holding the bottle in one hand by the narrow end, move the bottle in a swift, circular motion, watching as the water swirls in tornado fashion.

Note: You may want to glue the bottle cap on, or put masking tape around it, to ensure that the child cannot open it.

GROUP SIZE:

2–4 children

Ultimate Egg Tester

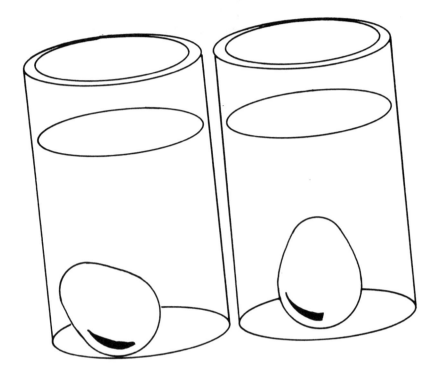

AGES: 3–5

DEVELOPMENTAL GOALS:

- ✂ To make comparisons
- ✂ To identify eggs that are fresh

LEARNING OBJECTIVE:

Using cups, water, fresh eggs, and eggs that have passed their expiration date, the child will test eggs to determine whether or not they are fresh.

MATERIALS:

Old eggs (several weeks beyond expiration date)
Fresh eggs
16-ounce cups
Water
Child-size pitcher

ADULT PREPARATION:

1. Separate old eggs (those with past-due expiration dates) from fresh eggs. Do not boil any of the eggs.
2. Pour water in a child-size pitcher.

PROCEDURES:

The child will complete the following steps:

1. Pour water into two cups, filling each two-thirds full.
2. Gently place an old egg in one cup.
3. Gently place a fresh egg in the other cup.
4. Observe that the fresh egg is lying horizontally on the bottom of its cup and the old egg is standing vertically (on one end) in its cup when asked, "Are the eggs sitting the same way or differently?"
5. Wash hands with soap and water after handling raw eggs.

continued

Ultimate Egg Tester continued

Notes: Explain to children that, as an egg deteriorates, air enters through its shell. When enough air is inside the egg, it will float. The Ultimate Egg Tester is a tried-and-true freshness test. Fresh eggs sink, and floating eggs should be thrown away.

GROUP SIZE:

2–5 children

Umbrella

DEVELOPMENTAL GOALS:

- ✂ To make predictions
- ✂ To improve eye-hand coordination

LEARNING OBJECTIVE:

Using a paper umbrella, a nylon or plastic umbrella, water, and an eyedropper, the child will test the effects of water on different types of material.

MATERIALS:

Child-size nylon or plastic umbrella
Paper umbrella from party store (one for each child)
Sensory table or large tub
Cups
Water
Eyedroppers or misting bottles

ADULT PREPARATION:

1. Empty and clean sensory table.
2. Place open child-size umbrella and an open paper umbrella in the sensory table or large tub.
3. Fill cups with water. (If children are too young to use eyedroppers, put the water in a spray bottle.)
4. Place the cups and eyedroppers with the umbrellas.

PROCEDURES:

1. Ask the children, "What kind of umbrella would you like to use in the rain?"
2. Ask the children, "What will happen when it rains on the paper umbrella?" and "What will happen when it rains on the nylon umbrella?"
3. Using the eyedroppers, the children sprinkle water on the umbrellas.

continued

Umbrella continued

4. When they have finished, ask the children, "What happened to the umbrellas?"

5. Explain that the nylon or plastic will repel the water, causing it to run off the umbrella, but the paper umbrella will absorb the water and eventually tear.

GROUP SIZE:

2–4 children

Vibrations

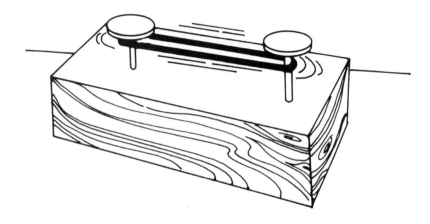

AGES: 3–5

DEVELOPMENTAL GOALS:

✄ To improve auditory discrimination

✄ To experience vibrations

LEARNING OBJECTIVE:

Using rubber bands, a fork, and a wooden block with nails, the child will create vibrations.

MATERIALS:

Rubber bands
Block of wood
Sandpaper
Child-size hammer
Goggles
Nails
Forks

ADULT PREPARATION:

1. Sand a block of wood or use one that has already been sanded.
2. Wearing goggles, hammer two nails into the block of wood, one near each end.
3. Stretch a rubber band between the nails.

PROCEDURES:

1. Show the child the block with the rubber band.
2. Ask, "What do you hear?"
3. Pull the rubber band and release them.
4. Ask, "What do you hear now?"
5. Show the child a fork.
6. Hold the fork, prongs upright, near the child's ear.
7. Ask, "What do you hear?"
8. Hit the fork on the table and then hold the fork, prongs upright, near the child's ear.

continued

Vibrations continued

9. Ask, "What do you hear now?"

10. Explain that the rubber band and the fork are vibrating, which creates sound waves that we hear.

GROUP SIZE:

3–4 children

Volcano

AGES: 2–5 years

DEVELOPMENTAL GOALS:

✂ To observe chemical reactions

✂ To increase fine motor skills

LEARNING OBJECTIVE:

Using a jar, baking soda, spoon, red coloring, and vinegar, the child will simulate a volcanic reaction.

MATERIALS:

Tall, narrow jar or vase
Tray
Baking soda
Spoon
Red food coloring or red liquid watercolor
Bowl
Water
Eyedropper
Measuring spoon (tablespoon)
Vinegar
Towels for cleanup
Child-size pitcher
Smocks

ADULT PREPARATION:

1. Put red coloring in a small bowl.
2. Add 2 tablespoons of water and stir well.
3. Put the vase or jar on a tray to catch the overflow.
4. Pour vinegar into a child-size pitcher.

PROCEDURES:

The child will complete the following steps:

1. Put a heaping spoonful of baking soda into the jar.
2. Using an eyedropper, add several drops of red coloring to simulate hot lava.
3. Using the child-size pitcher, pour vinegar into the jar, until a reaction is seen.
4. Watch as the baking soda and vinegar erupt over the top of the jar, spilling down the sides.

continued

Volcano continued

Notes: The reaction is caused by the creation of a gas when vinegar and baking soda are mixed together.

For children who are unable to use an eyedropper, put the coloring into a small squeeze bottle.

GROUP SIZE:

2–5 children

Water Current

DEVELOPMENTAL GOALS:

✂ To observe the effects of moving water

✂ To enhance large muscle development

LEARNING OBJECTIVE:

Using a sensory table, balls, and water, the child will observe the effects of moving water.

MATERIALS:

Sensory table or large plastic tub
Assortment of small balls
Water
Paper towels to dry hands

ADULT PREPARATION:

1. Pour water into the sensory table or a large plastic tub, filling it one-fourth to one-half full.
2. Cover the surface of the water with small balls that vary in size and texture.

PROCEDURES:

1. Ask children, "What will happen to the balls if we move our hands through the water in one direction?"
2. Have children run their hands through the water in a clockwise position, making large circular motions in the tub.
3. Point out that the balls are following the current they have generated.
4. Ask, "What will happen to the balls if we move our hands in the opposite direction?"

continued

Water Current continued

5. Show children how to run their hands through the water in a counterclockwise motion, making large circles in the tub.

6. Discuss how the balls jammed together at first, when the current changed direction, and then followed the counterclockwise current.

GROUP SIZE:

2 children

Water and Weight

ADULT PREPARATION:

1. Fill a large, clear bowl or container half full of water.
2. Mark the water level with masking tape.
3. Spread out towel to receive wet items.

PROCEDURES:

The child will complete the following steps:

1. Place a large rock in the water and observe how the water level rises.
2. Remove the rock and place an unopened can of food in the water. Again note the change in water level.
3. Repeat with the water bottle.

Note: The water will rise equal to the weight that displaces it.

GROUP SIZE:

3–5 children

DEVELOPMENTAL GOALS:

- ✂ To make comparisons
- ✂ To improve muscular coordination

LEARNING OBJECTIVE:

Using a bowl, tape, water, rocks, can of food, and bottle, the child will observe displacement of water when rocks are added to it.

MATERIALS:

Large, clear bowl or container
Water
Rocks
Unopened can of food
Bottle, filled with water
Masking tape
Towel

Weather Chart

AGES: 2–5

DEVELOPMENTAL GOALS:

✄ To observe the environment

✄ To record the weather

LEARNING OBJECTIVE:

Using a weather graph, symbols, and glue, the child will record the weather.

MATERIALS:

Copies of weather chart and symbols

Tape or white school glue

Scissors

ADULT PREPARATION:

1. Make a copy of the weather chart and several copies of each symbol for each child.

PROCEDURES:

1. If possible, have the children look outside.
2. Ask, "What kind of weather are we having today?"
3. Have the children select the symbol that resembles today's weather (sunny, rainy, cloudy, or snowy).
4. Have the children tape or glue that symbol in the first row of the chart, under the correct day of the week.
5. Repeat activity daily.

Note: This may be done using individual or group weather charts. The class chart may be enlarged and laminated, with hook and loop tape or masking tape used to affix the symbols.

GROUP SIZE:

2–10 children

continued

Weather Chart continued

Weather Chart				
Monday	Tuesday	Wednesday	Thursday	Friday

continued

Weather Chart continued

Weather Chart

Wet and Dry

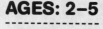

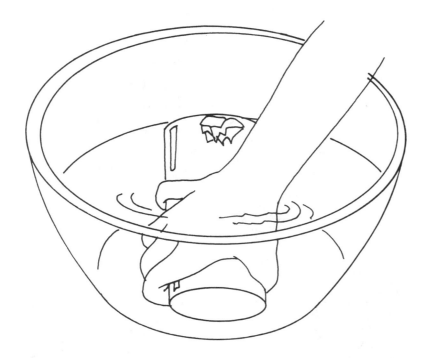

DEVELOPMENTAL GOALS:

✂ To improve observation skills

✂ To improve muscular coordination

LEARNING OBJECTIVE:

Using a cup, paper towel, water, and large bowl, the child will demonstrate the effects of air on water.

MATERIALS:

Small plastic cup
Paper towels or tissues
Large clear bowl
Water

ADULT PREPARATION:

1. Fill a clear bowl half full of water (enough water to totally submerge the cup).

PROCEDURES:

The child will complete the following steps:

1. Fold or crumple a paper towel and push it into the bottom of the cup.
2. Turn the cup upside down and push it straight to the bottom of the bowl.
3. Bring the cup straight up out of the bowl of water.
4. Take the paper towel out of the cup and feel it, observing that it is still dry.

Note: Explain that holding the cup upside down creates an air pocket that keeps water out of the cup. (If the towel became wet, the cup was not held straight.)

GROUP SIZE:

2 children

Whitening Teeth

DEVELOPMENTAL GOALS:

✄ To understand the concept of personal hygiene

✄ To observe transformations

LEARNING OBJECTIVE:

Using boiled eggs, cups, tea, toothbrush, and toothpaste, the child will demonstrate the effects of brushing teeth.

MATERIALS:

Boiled eggs (one for each child)
Pan
Water
Regular black tea
Cups (one for each child)
Toothbrush
Toothpaste
Permanent marker
Towel
Child-size pitcher

ADULT PREPARATION:

1. Boil eggs and set them aside to cool.
2. Make tea according to package directions.
3. Put the tea in a child-size pitcher.
4. Write each child's name on an individual cup.

PROCEDURES (DAY 1):

1. The children will place the boiled eggs in individual cups.
2. Using the child-size pitcher, the children will take turns pouring tea to cover the eggs.
3. Allow the eggs to sit in the tea at least 24 hours.

PROCEDURES (DAY 2):

1. Spread towel on the table.
2. Take eggs out of the tea and place on the towel.

continued

Whitening Teeth continued

3. Using toothbrushes and toothpaste, the children will attempt to clean the tea stains off the eggs.

Note: Relate this activity to the importance of brushing teeth.

 SAFETY PRECAUTION:

Children must always wash their hands after handling eggs.

GROUP SIZE:

2–4 children

Yeast

AGES: 3–5

DEVELOPMENTAL GOALS:

✄ To practice measuring

✄ To make comparisons

LEARNING OBJECTIVE:

Using resealable plastic bags, measuring spoons, yeast, sugar, and warm water, the child will observe the effects of mixing ingredients.

MATERIALS:

Resealable freezer plastic bags (pint or sandwich size—two for each experiment)
Measuring spoons
Small containers or bowls
Yeast
Sugar
Candy thermometer
Permanent marker
Microwave
Towel

ADULT PREPARATION:

1. Put sugar and yeast into small containers or bowls.
2. Write *sugar* on one resealable plastic bag with a permanent marker.
3. Write *no sugar* on the other resealable plastic bag.
4. Heat a cup of water for one minute in the microwave.
5. Using a thermometer, measure the temperature of the water, which should be 110 degrees.

PROCEDURES:

The child will complete the following steps:

1. With adult holding the bag open, measure and add 2 teaspoons of yeast to each bag.
2. Measure and add 1 teaspoon of sugar to only the bag marked *sugar*.
3. Measure and pour 4 tablespoons of warm water into each bag.
4. Watch as adult seals the bags securely.

continued

Yeast continued

5. Shake and squish the bags, mixing the ingredients together.

6. Set the bags on a towel.

7. Watch as the yeast and sugar mixture begins to rise in its bag (within five minutes).

8. Observe that there is no change in the mixture without sugar.

Note: Within 15 minutes, the yeast and sugar mixture will fill its bag. After 20 minutes, the bag will pop open.

GROUP SIZE:

2–4 children

Zipper Bag Color Mix

AGES: 1–5

DEVELOPMENTAL GOALS:

✂ To understand color mixing

✂ To recognize colors

LEARNING OBJECTIVE:

Using a resealable plastic bag; shaving cream; and red, blue, and yellow food coloring, the child will mix colors.

MATERIALS:

Plastic zipper bag (sandwich size—one for each child)

Shaving cream

Primary liquid water-colors or food coloring (blue, red, yellow)

Smock

Optional: packaging tape

ADULT PREPARATION:

1. Fill a plastic zipper bag half full of shaving cream.

PROCEDURES:

The child will complete the following steps:

1. Wearing a smock, choose and identify two different colors of liquid watercolor or food coloring.

2. Squirt the two colors into the bag of shaving cream.

3. With adult help, seal the bag.

4. Knead the outside of the bag until the colors have mixed and stained the shaving cream thoroughly.

5. Identify the new color made by blending two colors.

Note: If the bag is to be sent home, you may want to seal the top of the bag with packaging tape.

GROUP SIZE:

2–4 children

Zipper Bag Garden

AGES: 2–5

DEVELOPMENTAL GOALS:

- ✂ To promote gardening skills
- ✂ To observe the growth of a plant

LEARNING OBJECTIVE:

Using a resealable plastic bag, dried lima beans, paper towels, and water, the child will watch a plant grow.

MATERIALS:

Plastic zipper bags (one for each child)
Dried lima beans (four for each child)
Two bowls
Paper towels (one for each child)
Water

ADULT PREPARATION:

1. Put water in a bowl.
2. Put lima beans in a bowl.

PROCEDURES:

The child will complete the following steps:

1. Dip a paper towel in water and (with adult's help) squeeze out the excess.
2. Count out four lima beans.
3. Wrap lima beans in damp paper towel.
4. Put the paper towel in a resealable plastic bag.
5. With adult help, seal the bag.
6. Check the bag daily to see when the seeds begin to sprout.

continued

Zipper Bag Garden continued

⚠ SAFETY PRECAUTION:

Observe children closely. Lima beans may present a choking hazard for younger children.

GROUP SIZE:

2–4 children

Appendix A: Sensory Table

A sensory table is a necessity for preschool science. If you are performing these activities at home or are working at a center with a very small budget, a large plastic container may be used. Be sure to use a container with a lid if you want to store the sensory contents; the lid will keep the contents cleaner and make storage easier.

Sensory tables may be purchased from a school supply store or catalog in a wide range of prices. If possible, select one with a lid. Covering the sensory table not only keeps the contents cleaner but also maximizes space, because a sensory table with a lid can do double duty as a science table. When purchasing a table you may want to select one that has a drainage plug in the bottom for easy cleanup. You may also want one that is on wheels, enabling you to move the table for outside use or cleaning.

Hygiene is very important when using a sensory table. Children need to wash their hands before participating at the table, because unwashed hands may deposit germs into the sand or other filler. Then the next child who uses the table may extract those germs. During cold and flu season, you will want to change the contents of the sensory table more often. If you are using water, drain and dry the container daily.

When using sand in the sensory table you may want to moisten it. Damp sand works best for molding. Be careful to dry the sand by leaving the lid off the table when the children are not in the classroom. Keeping the cover on damp sand causes mold to grow.

Vary materials in the sensory table. In warmer weather, we put water in the table. Other fillers include confetti, corn meal, corn, cotton balls, dry beans, Easter-basket grass, grits, lima beans, marbles, oatmeal, packing peanuts, popcorn, rice, sand, and shredded paper. We have also used various materials to go along with our "letter of the week" exercises.

The following alphabetical list gives some suggestions for items and appropriate activities to use with a sensory table. Please use a choking tube to determine whether or not these items should be used with children younger than three. Items that will slip through the tube may present a choking hazard for young children.

Appendix B: Sensory Table Activities

Letter	Materials
A	Use shredded paper as filler. Hide and search for small plastic *apples*. Add small pails to gather the *apples*. *Acorns* can be put in with fall leaves and pine cones. The *acorns* may also be hidden and searched for in shredded paper or silk leaves.
B	Put small *balls* in water. Push the *balls* to the bottom of the table and release. The *balls* will pop back up to the top. Use dry *beans* as filler. Search for small counter *bears* and *buttons* in the beans. Draw faces on lima *beans* with a permanent marker, making them resemble ghosts. Use tweezers and small bowls to collect the ghosts.
C	Hide and search for *candy canes*. Use green and red packing grass as filler. Hide one *candy cane* for each child. Use shelled *corn* as filler. Use *cotton balls* as filler. Hide foam snowflakes during a winter unit. Children may search through the *cotton balls* for the snowflakes wearing mittens.
D	Hide plastic *dinosaurs* in sand or corn meal. Tint water blue as filler. Float plastic *ducks* on the water.
E	Hide and search for plastic *eggs* in Easter grass. Supply baskets to put the *eggs* in. Use water as filler. Float small plastic containers in the water. Using *eyedroppers*, have the children put water into the containers to see if they can be filled with enough water to cause them to sink.
F	Hide and search for *feathers* hidden in a filler of corn, beans, or rice. *Film canisters* may be used to scoop up sand, rice, or grits. Place plastic *fish* in water that is tinted blue. Supply a *fish net* to capture the *fish*.

Letter	Materials
G	Search for *gold*. Spray paint rocks *gold*. Hide them in a dry filler and have children find the *gold*. Supply a black pot to put the collected *gold* into. This is a great activity for a St. Patrick's Day unit. Use *grits* as filler. Spoons, measuring cups of various sizes, and funnels may be used to manipulate and measure the *grits*.
H	Purchase foam *hearts* or jeweled *hearts* from a dollar store or craft store. Hide and search for the *hearts* in Easter grass or shredded paper. Use sand as filler. A spoon may be used to make trails through the sand. Place plastic *horses* on the trails. Cut various lengths of a garden *hose*. Use water as the filler. Dip the *hose* in water, lift it, and watch the water run out of both ends. Tip the *hose* and the water will run out of one end.
I	Place *ice cubes* in the sensory table and have children wear mittens to move or stack the *ice*. Small shovels and buckets may also be used to manipulate the *ice cubes*. Hide plastic *insects* in Easter grass or shredded paper. Tweezers may be used to pick up the *insects*.
J	Using Easter grass as filler, hide and search for plastic *jelly beans*. Hide and search for *jingle bells* in cotton balls or shredded paper.
K	Hide and search for *keys* in a dry filler.
L	Use real, silk, or paper (cutout) *leaves* as filler. Use dry *lima beans* as filler. It is very soothing to run the hands through these beans. Hide and search for wrapped *lollipops* in a loose filler such as shredded paper or corn. Hide one for each child.
M	Search for *magnetic* items in shredded paper with the *magnetic wand*. Hide and search for *marbles* in a filler.
N	Put mixed *nuts* (still in the shell) into water and use a small *net* to capture the *nuts*. Hide and search for *nuts and bolts* in a lightweight filler such as shredded paper or Easter grass. Use a magnet to search for these metal objects.
O	Fill the table with *oatmeal*. Use cups, funnels, and spoons to move and measure the *oatmeal*.
P	Use *packing peanuts* as filler. Hide and search for items that are *purple* and *pink*. Use tongs to move *packing peanuts* or hidden items from one side of the table to the other.

SENSORY TABLE ACTIVITIES (continued)

Letter	Materials
Q	Hide *queens* from several decks of cards in a dry filler. Hide and search for *quarters* in dry filler.
R	Put tinted *rice* as filler in the table. Tint the rice by putting it into gallon-size resealable plastic bags. Fill the bags half full of rice. Add one capful of rubbing alcohol mixed with liquid watercolor or food coloring—use enough coloring to achieve the hue desired. Shake the bag, mixing the color thoroughly throughout the rice. Use a different color in each bag. Lay the rice on newspaper until dry, then put into sensory table. Hide and search for *ribbons* of various colors and lengths in a filler.
S	Bury and search for *seashells* in the *sand*. Make *soapy water* by adding dish soap to water. Use a whisk or eggbeater to create bubbles. Add dishes and a washcloth to wash the dishes.
T	Tear *tissue paper* into pieces. Hide and search for items that begin with the letter *T*.
U	Make a beach scene with sand, shells, and small paper *umbrellas*.
V	Hide and search for *valentines* in a dry filler.
W	Use a *water wheel* or *watering can* in water. Hide plastic fishing *worms* (without hooks) in sand. Use a small shovel and can to collect the *worms*.
X	Hide and search for cutout *X*s in a dry filler. Laminate the *X*s before using.
Y	Place scraps of *yarn* in the table. Hide *yellow* objects to search for in the *yarn*.
Z	Create a *zoo* with plastic animals. Use craft sticks to make fences.

Index by Science Concepts

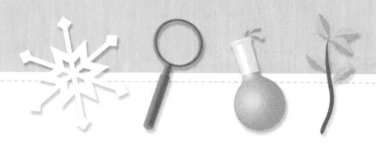

Index by Units

Index

Ms. Thomas

Science Activities A to Z

Joanne Matricardi and Jeanne McLarty

Presented in a detailed lesson plan format, Science Activities A to Z offers a plethora of science activities for young children ages one and up. The activities are easy-to-understand and follow—making them enjoyable for teachers, parents and children. Each section helps teachers and parents find science activities for a theme-based curriculum incorporating a letter of the week. The many activities given for each targeted alphabet letter offer a host of teaching options. A theme-specific index and a science-concept index make it easy to find just the right activities for each lesson.

Key Features:

- Helpful hints give tried-and-true suggestions to make the science experience easier and more enjoyable
- Lesson plan format provides detailed plans in an easy-to-read, organized format
- The variety of choices within each alphabet letter helps a teacher complete a years' worth of science activities
- Age appropriateness of the activities helps educators in making plans based on the children's ages

"I think Science Activities A to Z is a great book! It is not intimidating as many science activity books can be and the directions are clear and easy to follow. When the experiments are fun and interesting for the teacher or parent, they are likely to be successful activities for the children as well."

— Brenda Schin, Private Child Care, Ballston Spa, NY

"I would definitely purchase this product for my teachers because it is very hands-on which is something we require in our curriculum. I found the organization of the book to be extremely effective and the level of detail to be just the right amount. The activities were appropriate for a child care center setting."

— Mary Hornbeck, Executive Director/Owner, Special Beginnings Early Learning Center

Other Titles Available in the A to Z Series:

Art Activities A to Z
ISBN: 1-4018-7164-X

Cooking Activities A to Z
ISBN: 1-4018-7239-5

Group Time Activities A to Z
ISBN: 1-4018-7237-9

Math Activities A to Z
ISBN: 1-4018-7235-2

Patterns for Activities A to Z
ISBN: 1-4018-7241-7

THOMSON

DELMAR LEARNING

Visit www.earlychilded.delmar.com or www.delmarlearning.com
for your lifelong learning solutions.

ISBN-13: 978-1-4018-7232-8
ISBN-10: 1-4018-7232-8

90000

9 781401 872328